SOUTH AFRICA

SOUTH AFRICA

1880 TO THE PRESENT:
IMPERIALISM, NATIONALISM, AND APARTHEID

BRUCE AND BECKY DUROST FISH

INTRODUCTORY ESSAY BY
Dr. Richard E. Leakey
Chairman, Wildlife Clubs
of Kenya Association
✛
AFTERWORD BY
Deirdre Shields

CHELSEA HOUSE PUBLISHERS
Philadelphia
In association with Covos Day Books, South Africa

CHELSEA HOUSE PUBLISHERS

EDITOR IN CHIEF Stephen Reginald
PRODUCTION MANAGER Pamela Loos
ART DIRECTOR Sara Davis
PICTURE EDITOR Judy L. Hasday
MANAGING EDITOR James D. Gallagher
SENIOR PRODUCTION EDITOR LeeAnne Gelletly
ASSOCIATE ART DIRECTOR Takeshi Takahashi
SERIES DESIGNER Keith Trego
COVER DESIGN Emiliano Begnardi

First Printing
1 3 5 7 9 8 6 4 2

Library of Congress Cataloging-in-Publication Data

Fish, Bruce.
        South Africa / by Bruce and Becky Durost Fish.
                p.   cm. — (Exploration of Africa, the emerging nations)
        Includes bibliographical references and index.
        Summary: Examines the past, development, inhabitants, and many
        cultural aspects of South Africa.
        ISBN 0-7910-5676-7
        1. South Africa—Juvenile literature. [1. South Africa.] I. Fish,
        Becky Durost. II. Title. III. Series.
        DT1719.F57 2000
        968—dc21

                                            99-058748

The photographs in this book are from the Royal Geographical Society Picture Library. Most are being published for the first time.

The Royal Geographical Society Picture Library provides an unrivaled source of over half a million images of peoples and landscapes from around the globe. Photographs date from the 1840s onwards on a variety of subjects including the British Colonial Empire, deserts, exploration, indigenous peoples, landscapes, remote destinations, and travel.

Photography, beginning with the daguerreotype in 1839, is only marginally younger than the Society, which encouraged its explorers to use the new medium from its earliest days. From the remarkable mid-19th century black-and-white photographs to color transparencies of the late 20th century, the focus of the collection is not the generic stock shot but the portrayal of man's resilience, adaptability and mobility in remote parts of the world.

In organizing this project, we have incurred many debts of gratitude. Our first, though, is to the professional staff of the Picture Library for their generous assistance, especially to Joanna Scadden, Picture Library Manager.

CONTENTS

Exploration of Africa: The Emerging Nations

THE DARK CONTINENT

DR. RICHARD E. LEAKEY

THE CONCEPT OF AFRICAN exploration has been greatly influenced by the hero status given to the European adventurers and missionaries who went off to Africa in the last century. Their travels and travails were certainly extraordinary and nobody can help but be impressed by the tremendous physical and intellectual courage that was so much a characteristic of people such as Livingstone, Stanley, Speke, and Baker, to name just a few. The challenges and rewards that Africa offered, both in terms of commerce and also "saved souls," inspired people to take incredible risks and endure personal suffering to a degree that was probably unique to the exploration of Africa.

I myself was fortunate enough to have had the opportunity to organize one or two minor expeditions to remote spots in Africa where there were no roads or airfields and marching with porters and/or camels was the best option at the time. I have also had the thrill of being with people untouched and often unmoved by contact with Western or other technologically based cultures, and these experiences remain for me amongst the most exciting and salutary of my life. With the contemporary revolution in technology, there will be few if any such opportunities again. Indeed I often find myself slightly saddened by the realization that were life ever discovered on another planet, exploration would doubtless be done by remote sensing and making full use of artificial, digital intelligence. At least it is unlikely to be in my lifetime and this is a relief!

INTRODUCTION

Notwithstanding all of this, I believe that the age of exploration and discovery in Africa is far from over. The future offers incredible opportunities for new discoveries that will push back the frontiers of knowledge. This endeavor will of course not involve exotic and arduous journeys into malaria-infested tropical swamps, but it will certainly require dedication, team work, public support, and a conviction that the rewards to be gained will more than justify the efforts and investment.

EARLY EXPLORERS

Many of us were raised and educated at school with the belief that Africa, the so-called Dark Continent, was actually discovered by early European travelers and explorers. The date of this "discovery" is difficult to establish, and anyway a distinction has always had to be drawn between northern Africa and the vast area south of the Sahara. The Romans certainly had information about the continent's interior as did others such as the Greeks. A diverse range of traders ventured down both the west coast and the east coast from at least the ninth century, and by the tenth century Islam had taken root in a number of new towns and settlements established by Persian and Arab interests along the eastern tropical shores. Trans-African trade was probably under way well before this time, perhaps partly stimulated by external interests.

Close to the beginning of the first millennium, early Christians were establishing the Coptic church in the ancient kingdom of Ethiopia and at other coastal settlements along Africa's northern Mediterranean coast. Along the west coast of Africa, European trade in gold, ivory, and people was well established by the sixteenth century. Several hundred years later, early in the 19th century, the systematic penetration and geographical exploration of Africa was undertaken by Europeans seeking geographical knowledge and territory and looking for opportunities not only for commerce but for the chance to spread the Gospel. The extraordinary narratives of some of the journeys of early European travelers and adventurers in Africa are a vivid reminder of just how recently Africa has become embroiled in the power struggles and vested interests of non-Africans.

THE DARK CONTINENT

AFRICA'S GIFT TO THE WORLD

My own preoccupation over the past thirty years has been to study human prehistory, and from this perspective it is very clear that Africa was never "discovered" in the sense in which so many people have been and, perhaps, still are being taught. Rather, it was Africans themselves who found that there was a world beyond their shores. Prior to about two million years ago, the only humans or proto-humans in existence were confined to Africa; as yet, the remaining world had not been exposed to this strange mammalian species, which in time came to dominate the entire planet. It is no trivial matter to recognize the cultural implications that arise from this entirely different perspective of Africa and its relationship to the rest of humanity.

How many of the world's population grow up knowing that it was in fact African people who first moved and settled in southern Europe and Central Asia and migrated to the Far East? How many know that Africa's principal contribution to the world is in fact humanity itself? These concepts are quite different from the notion that Africa was only "discovered" in the past few hundred years and will surely change the commonly held idea that somehow Africa is a "laggard," late to come onto the world stage.

It could be argued that our early human forebears—the *Homo erectus* who moved out of Africa—have little or no bearing on the contemporary world and its problems. I disagree and believe that the often pejorative thoughts that are associated with the Dark Continent and dark skins, as well as with the general sense that Africans are somehow outside the mainstream of human achievement, would be entirely negated by the full acceptance of a universal African heritage for all of humanity. This, after all, is the truth that has now been firmly established by scientific inquiry.

The study of human origins and prehistory will surely continue to be important in a number of regions of Africa and this research must continue to rank high on the list of relevant ongoing exploration and discovery. There is still much to be learned about the early stages of human development, and the age of the "first humans"—the first bipedal apes—has not been firmly established. The current hypothesis is that prior to five million years ago there were no bipeds, and this would mean that humankind is only five million years old. Beyond Africa, there were no humans until just two million years ago, and this is a consideration that political leaders and people as a whole need to bear in mind.

Recent History

When it comes to the relatively recent history of Africa's contemporary people, there is still considerable ignorance. The evidence suggests that there were major migrations of people within the continent during the past 5,000 years, and the impact of the introduction of domestic stock must have been quite considerable on the way of life of many of Africa's people. Early settlements and the beginnings of nation states are, as yet, poorly researched and recorded. Although archaeological studies have been undertaken in Africa for well over a hundred years, there remain more questions than answers.

One question of universal interest concerns the origin and inspiration for the civilization of early Egypt. The Nile has, of course, offered opportunities for contacts between the heart of Africa and the Mediterranean seacoast, but very little is known about human settlement and civilization in the upper reaches of the Blue and White Nile between 4,000 and 10,000 years ago. We do know that the present Sahara Desert is only about 10,000 years old; before this, Central Africa was wetter and more fertile, and research findings have shown that it was only during the past 10,000 years that Lake Turkana in the northern Kenya was isolated from the Nile system. When connected, it would have been an excellent connection between the heartland of the continent and the Mediterranean.

Another question focuses on the extensive stone-walled villages and towns in Southern Africa. The Great Zimbabwe is but one of thousands of standing monuments in East, Central, and Southern Africa that attest to considerable human endeavor in Africa long before contact with Europe or Arabia. The Neolithic period and Iron Age still offer very great opportunities for exploration and discovery.

As an example of the importance of history, let us look at the modern South Africa where a visitor might still be struck by the not-too-subtle representation of a past that, until a few years ago, only "began" with the arrival of Dutch settlers some 400 years back. There are, of course, many pre-Dutch sites, including extensive fortified towns where kingdoms and nation states had thrived hundreds of years before contact with Europe; but this evidence has been poorly documented and even more poorly portrayed.

Few need to be reminded of the sparseness of Africa's precolonial written history. There are countless cultures and historical narratives that have been recorded only as oral history and legend. As postcolonial Africa further consolidates itself, history must be reviewed and deepened to incorporate the realities of precolonial human settlement as well as foreign contact. Africa's identity and self-respect is closely linked to this.

One of the great tragedies is that African history was of little interest to the early European travelers who were in a hurry and had no brief to document the details of the people they came across during their travels. In the basements of countless European museums, there are stacked shelves of African "curios"—objects taken from the people but seldom documented in terms of the objects' use, customs, and history.

There is surely an opportunity here for contemporary scholars to do something. While much of Africa's precolonial past has been obscured by the slave trade, colonialism, evangelism, and modernization, there remains an opportunity, at least in some parts of the continent, to record what still exists. This has to be one of the most vital frontiers for African exploration and discovery as we begin a new millennium. Some of the work will require trips to the field, but great gains could be achieved by a systematic and coordinated effort to record the inventories of European museums and archives. The Royal Geographical Society could well play a leading role in this chapter of African exploration. The compilation of a central data bank on what is known and what exists would, if based on a coordinated initiative to record the customs and social organization of Africa's remaining indigenous peoples, be a huge contribution to the heritage of humankind.

MEDICINES AND FOODS

On the African continent itself, there remain countless other areas for exploration and discovery. Such endeavors will be achieved without the fanfare of great expeditions and high adventure as was the case during the last century and they should, as far as possible, involve

INTRODUCTION

exploration and discovery of African frontiers by Africans themselves. These frontiers are not geographic: they are boundaries of knowledge in the sphere of Africa's home-grown cultures and natural world.

Indigenous knowledge is a very poorly documented subject in many parts of the world, and Africa is a prime example of a continent where centuries of accumulated local knowledge is rapidly disappearing in the face of modernization. I believe, for example, that there is much to be learned about the use of wild African plants for both medicinal and nutritional purposes. Such knowledge, kept to a large extent as the experience and memory of elders in various indigenous communities, could potentially have far-reaching benefits for Africa and for humanity as a whole.

The importance of new remedies based on age-old medicines cannot be underestimated. Over the past two decades, international companies have begun to take note and to exploit certain African plants for pharmacological preparations. All too often, Africa has not been the beneficiary of these "discoveries," which are, in most instances, nothing more than the refinement and improvement of traditional African medicine. The opportunities for exploration and discovery in this area are immense and will have assured economic return on investment. One can only hope that such work will be in partnership with the people of Africa and not at the expense of the continent's best interests.

Within the same context, there is much to be learned about the traditional knowledge of the thousands of plants that have been utilized by different African communities for food. The contemporary world has become almost entirely dependent, in terms of staple foods, on the cultivation of only six principal plants: corn, wheat, rice, yams, potatoes, and bananas. This cannot be a secure basis to guarantee the food requirements of more than five billion people.

Many traditional food plants in Africa are drought resistant and might well offer new alternatives for large-scale agricultural development in the years to come. Crucial to this development is finding out what African people used before exotics were introduced. In some rural areas of the continent, it is still possible to learn about much of this by talking to the older generation. It is certainly a great shame that some of the early European travelers in Africa were ill equipped to study and record details of diet and traditional plant use, but I am sure that, although it is late, it is not too late. The compilation of a pan-African database on what is known about the use of the continent's plant resources is a vital matter requiring action.

VANISHING SPECIES

In the same spirit, there is as yet a very incomplete inventory of the continent's other species. The inevitable trend of bringing land into productive management is resulting in the loss of unknown but undoubtedly large numbers of species. This genetic resource may be invaluable to the future of Africa and indeed humankind, and there really is a need for coordinated efforts to record and understand the continent's biodiversity.

In recent years important advances have been made in the study of tropical ecosystems in Central and South America, and I am sure that similar endeavors in Africa would be rewarding. At present, Africa's semi-arid and highland ecosystems are better understood than the more diverse and complex lowland forests, which are themselves under particular threat from loggers and farmers. The challenges of exploring the biodiversity of the upper canopy in the tropical forests, using the same techniques that are now used in Central American forests, are fantastic and might also lead to eco-tourist developments for these areas in the future.

It is indeed an irony that huge amounts of money are being spent by the advanced nations in an effort to discover life beyond our own planet, while at the same time nobody on this planet knows the extent and variety of life here at home. The tropics are especially relevant in this regard and one can only hope that Africa will become the focus of renewed efforts of research on biodiversity and tropical ecology.

AN AFROCENTRIC VIEW

Overall, the history of Africa has been presented from an entirely Eurocentric or even Caucasocentric perspective, and until recently this has not been adequately reviewed. The penetration of Africa, especially during the last century, was important in its own way; but today the realities of African history, art, culture, and politics are better known. The time has come to regard African history in terms of what has happened in Africa itself, rather than simply in terms of what non-African individuals did when they first traveled to the continent.

Ancient San Art *Paintings and engravings on rocks are found extensively in southern Africa. Most of these works were probably done by ancestors of the San, the hunting/food gathering peoples of the region. The San rank among the oldest inhabitants of the planet earth.*

Seizing Victory from Defeat

Lieutenant-General Frederic Thesiger, second baron of Chelmsford, was stunned. Over a thousand of his most experienced men lay dead a few miles inside the western border of Zululand. The remainder of his forces had been forced to retreat so rapidly that there was not even time to bury the bodies.

What he had expected to be a quick and decisive military campaign had suddenly become one of the worst British defeats in the entire century. Many of his staff worried that he was on the verge of a breakdown.

No matter how often he examined the events of the past few days, Chelmsford couldn't understand how the British had been mauled so badly. On January 22, 1879, his troops, armed with modern rifles and rapid-firing field guns, had been overwhelmed by a Zulu force carrying only spears and a few outdated firearms.

Lord Carnarvon's "Forward" Policy for the British Empire

The roots of the disaster went back to 1876. At that time Lord Carnarvon was colonial secretary under British Prime Minister Benjamin Disraeli. For years Carnarvon had been an outspoken advocate of a "forward" policy for the British Empire. He wanted to push forward the boundaries of British territory throughout the world. In

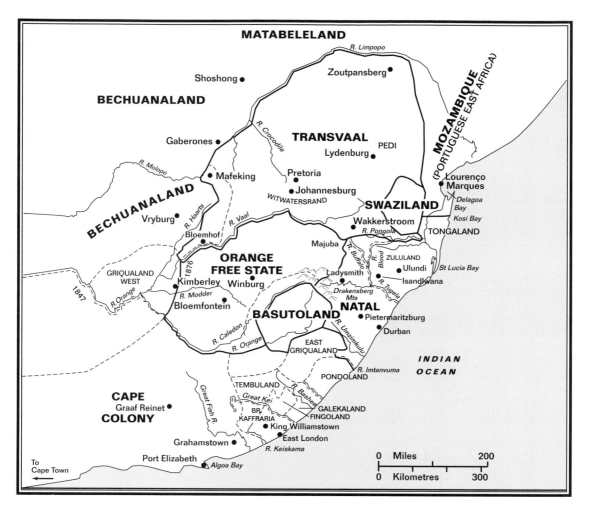

South Africa, 1877–1881

1867 he realized his greatest achievement—the passage of the British North American Act, which gave Canada its federal system and dominion status. In 1875 he proposed a South African federation based on the Canadian system.

Great Britain already controlled the Cape Colony, on the southern tip of Africa, and Natal, a region northeast of the Cape that bordered the Indian Ocean. But Lord Carnarvon dreamed of expanding these holdings to include all the territory between Cape Town and the Zambezi River, more than one thousand miles northeast. Standing in his way were several

African kingdoms as well as territories held by the descendants of Dutch Calvinist immigrants, a deeply religious and stubbornly in-dependent people. These Dutch settlers called themselves Afrikaners (people of Africa) or Boers, the Dutch word for farmer.

In 1876 Lord Carnarvon convinced Bartle Frere to become governor and high commissioner of the Cape Colony and gave him instructions to implement the planned confederation. Frere, whose experience as a colonial administrator was primarily in India, didn't know much about Africa, but he was excited about Carnarvon's vision for the British Empire. Frere soon discovered how audacious that vision could be.

When Frere arrived in Cape Town, he found it in turmoil. The British colonists were unsympathetic to Carnarvon's plan for shared authority with the Boers. Two weeks later, on April 12, 1877, the situation became even more complicated when Sir Theophilus Shepstone, misinterpreting orders from Lord Carnarvon, placed the Boers of Transvaal under British rule.

The Boers of the Transvaal

The Transvaal, which means "across the Vaal," had been settled in the 1830s by Afrikaners who were unhappy with life in the Cape Colony. After the British took over the Cape Colony and outlawed slavery, the Afrikaners moved north, taking 6,000 slaves with them. They crossed the Vaal River and created a new life for themselves. In the process, they enslaved Africans who already lived there and drove out many others. These "trekboers," as they were soon called by the larger Afrikaner community, developed a rural economy, established their own government, and disagreed continuously about what that government should do.

By the 1870s their disunity had produced grave financial problems and they were in no position to prevent the British from taking over. Theophilus Shepstone, accompanied by only 25 policemen, simply entered Pretoria, the capital of the Transvaal, and proclaimed the whole region a British possession.

Bartle Frere was left with the job of convincing the Boers to support a South African federation. They outnumbered the British in southern Africa by three to two, and he didn't want to see armed conflict between the Boer and British colonists. So the Boers were promised self-government within the Transvaal.

Frere knew that the Boers had another concern. Whites in the region were outnumbered by a vast majority of indigenous Africans. In the Transvaal and Natal, the ratio was at least ten to one. And both regions were bordered by Zululand, an African kingdom renowned for the leadership of its king, Cetshwayo, and the legendary prowess of his more than 30,000 warriors.

THE PERCEIVED ZULU THREAT

Frere relied on Shepstone for advice about the Zulus because he had lived among them for three decades. Success in dealing with Cetshwayo had led to Shepstone's promotion to Secretary of Native Affairs and had earned him a seat on the executive council of the newly created Natal Colony. Shepstone had previously championed a policy of respecting tribal land claims, but Frere now noticed a surprising change. Shepstone no longer supported the Zulus but spoke of a white union—the Boers and the British—against the Africans.

Shepstone collected reports from farmers and missionaries hostile to the Zulu king. He organized a campaign that portrayed Cetshwayo as a ruthless tyrant, a threat to British plans for controlling the region. Soon southern Africa, as well as the colonial office in London, was deluged with rumors of an imminent Zulu invasion of Natal. Missionaries were advised to leave Zululand. Together, Shepstone and Frere deliberately misrepresented the Zulu army as a menacing force.

In July 1878 a British commission reviewed a border dispute between the Boers and the Zulus. It ruled in favor of the Zulus. This decision made it more difficult for Frere to convince the Boers to accept Transvaal annexation and the British promise to protect them. It seemed that the Zulus had become an obstacle to federation between the various white peoples in southern Africa.

Frere, who was made a baronet for his work in promoting English domination in India, needed a way to eliminate the Zulu nation. Simply put, the Zulus were a threat to British expansionist plans.

THE BATTLE OF ISANDHLWANA

In December 1878, acting without the knowledge of his superiors, Frere provoked a crisis. He sent an ultimatum to King Cetshwayo: Missionaries had to be allowed back into Zululand (in fact they had never been forced out but had left because of the propaganda campaign waged by Shepstone and Frere); Zululand had to become a British protectorate; and the well-organized military system, which gave the king his power and was a central part of Zulu society, had to be disbanded. If the king did not comply with Frere's demands within 30 days, the British would invade.

On January 11, 1879, the time limit expired. Frere had his excuse for a war against the Zulus. Thus Chelmsford started his ill-fated campaign. A British army of more than 7,000 soldiers with some 1,000 white volunteers and 2,000 African mercenaries invaded Zululand from three directions.

Chelmsford intended for the three columns to strike Zululand together, driving the Zulus back to their capital city, Ulundi. He hoped to draw their warriors into a decisive battle on open ground, where superior British weapons could destroy them.

The central column, with Chelmsford in command, had approximately 1,600 British troops, a battery of six small field guns, as well as African soldiers and white volunteers. Altogether, the central column contained just under 4,000 fighting men.

Chelmsford expected to meet little or no resistance. In his only previous experience in fighting Africans, he had observed that they used hit-and-run attacks to harass large troop formations. He assumed that the Zulu warriors would use similar tactics.

He never took seriously the warnings he received from the Boers, who had spent decades fighting the Zulus. They described how large formations of Zulu warriors engaged and overwhelmed an enemy. They also stressed that King Cetshwayo's warriors were masters at disguising their movements. Once he had crossed into Zululand, Chelmsford sent out only a few scouts to discover his enemy's movements.

On January 20, Chelmsford's column camped on the eastern face of a gently sloping hill, in the shadow of a 300-foot-high rock outcropping, which the Zulus called Isandhlwana, "the little house."

Chelmsford didn't order trenches dug or other fortifications built. Because the supply wagons were difficult to maneuver, he didn't use them to create a line of defense—a precaution recommended by the Boers. Although they were counting on the massed firepower of the British infantry to stop any large Zulu attack, he and his officers failed to establish clear fields of fire. Nor did they stockpile ammunition at defensible points around the perimeter of the camp, in the event that soldiers were cut off from the supply wagons or had to keep up a rapid rate of fire for a prolonged period of time.

Before dawn on January 22, one of Chelmsford's few scouting parties sent word that it had spotted a large force of Zulus. With about 2,000 soldiers, Chelmsford quickly moved to intercept them. He called up reinforcements from his supply camp at Rorke's Drift on the Buffalo River, 12 miles west along a rough wagon road. When they arrived, 1,700 to 1,800 British, African, and white volunteer troops were available to defend the camp.

After hours of searching, Chelmsford's force had killed or captured fewer than 80 warriors. The lieutenant general was extremely irritated with these meager results. Then he received messages warning that a large Zulu force was attacking the main camp. He ignored the reports and ordered a few worried officers to remain with him.

Captured Zulu warriors insisted that about 20,000 men had been sent to defeat him. Still, Chelmsford wasn't concerned. Some of his officers were even amused by the idea that their base camp might be attacked.

By three o'clock that afternoon, Chelmsford was convinced that the Zulus he was pursuing had slipped away. He ordered his troops to turn around. On the way back to camp, they were met by the white commander of an African battalion loyal to the British. When he had returned to camp earlier in the afternoon, a sentry had fired at him. Startled, he suddenly realized that the traditional red coats of the British army that he saw around him were all covering black bodies! There wasn't another white man in sight. Zulu warriors were looting the main camp.

Chelmsford understood then the magnitude of his folly. He assembled his men and prepared to retake the camp. By the time they reached it, the Zulus had withdrawn. All that remained were their dead comrades.

For hours, Chelmsford waited amid the gruesome carnage, deliberating what to do. Finally, he decided to retreat.

The British failure to defend their encampment, a basic principle in warfare, had led to the loss of between 1,400 and 1,500 soldiers. This near obliteration of a British force had been accomplished by more than 20,000 Zulu warriors who had advanced undetected. The cost to the Zulus was also very high. Over 2,000 men were killed in the battle and hundreds more died from terrible wounds.

The losses at the Battle of Isandhlwana (January 22–23, 1879) astonished the British. Prime Minister Disraeli immediately sent Sir Garnet Wolseley to replace Frere as high commissioner, with authority to take over command of the army from Chelmsford. Wolseley, at 25, was the youngest colonel in the British army. He had a sterling reputation as a highly efficient commander. In England his adoring public carefully noted how successive governments used him as chief troubleshooter for the British Empire.

The Zulu War dragged on during the several months it took Wolseley to get to southern Africa. With the help of reinforcements, Chelmsford managed to blunder his way to a British victory at Ulundi, the Zulu capital (July 4, 1879). Wolseley arrived in time to accept the surrender of Cetshwayo.

Wolseley's most important achievement was the division of Zululand into 13 miniature states, each ruled by a different chief. The chiefs soon began fighting among themselves, making it impossible for them to take any united action against either the British or the Boers. The division of Zululand was a classic case of the destruction of a nation achieved by the policy of divide and conquer.

THE BOER UPRISING

The Boers, however, were not satisfied. The Zulus were still free from direct British rule, whereas the Boers in the Transvaal saw the Union Jack flying over their capital city every day. That flag symbolized everything they hated about British control.

As high commissioner, Wolseley was determined to dominate the Boers. He believed they were cowards and he ignored all warnings about their growing passion for independence from the British. He could not comprehend that fellow white people might despise the British more than they feared life in the midst of a vastly larger African population.

With the defeat of the Zulus, a major threat to British expansion in Africa had been eliminated. But it took time for the British public to see the Zulu War as a victory. It took even longer for them to respect the Boers' desire for freedom.

The situation in southern Africa contributed to Prime Minister Benjamin Disraeli's defeat in the next general election in Britain. In March 1880 his Conservative party was replaced by the Liberals under William Gladstone.

While campaigning for office, Gladstone promised independence for the Boers. After he became prime minister, however, he flatly rejected their request for a nation of their own.

Boer Family, Ghanzi, West Central Botswana, c. 1920 *The Boers are South Africans of Dutch, German, and French Huguenot descent. For the most part, almost all Boers trace their ancestry to the 1707 enumeration conducted by the Dutch East India Company's Cape Colony. Today, their descendants are commonly referred to as Afrikaners. The Boers developed their own subculture based on self-sufficient patriarchal communities. Staunch Calvinists, they saw themselves as the children of God in the wilderness, a Christian elect, divinely ordained to rule the land, including the natives whom they considered backward and inferior. By the end of the 18th century, the Boers spoke Afrikaans, which had diverged sufficiently from Dutch to be considered a separate language.*

Ghanzi was the starting point of a 500-mile cattle trek southward across the Kalahari Desert to the slaughterhouses at Lobatse. In 1898 large land grants were given to the Boers. Until the 1960s they led a life of virtual isolation. Many of their descendants still occupy the same farms today.

In April 1880 Garnet Wolseley happily returned to England and Major-General George Colley took over command of all British forces in southern Africa. Wolseley's only regret was that he had not had an opportunity to prove the superiority of British arms and British civilization by crushing the Boers.

The British continued to assume that the Boers were too weak and divided to ever take up arms against them. This was a grave miscalculation. While these hardy farmers had shown an amazing ability to fight among themselves, their shared grievances against the British were drawing them closer together. An event in 1880 brought that unification process to a rapid completion. The British insisted that the Boers pay taxes.

To no one's surprise, except the British, most Boers refused. In November 1880 when a local British sheriff seized a farmer's wagons to cover the latter's tax bill, armed Boers immediately recaptured the wagons and returned them to their owner. Boers throughout the region were outraged.

In early December 1880 thousands of Boers gathered to show their support for independence. More than 5,000 armed volunteers—skilled hunters and battle-hardened by years of conflict with Africans—took an oath to defeat the British.

On December 16, 1880, these Boers proclaimed their independence from Great Britain. They raised the *vierkleur,* the orange, red, white, and blue flag of the new South African Republic.

Four days later about 150 armed Boers rode out to meet two companies of the British 94th regiment who had been sent to suppress the rebellion. The nine British officers and 248 enlisted men were less than a two-day march from Pretoria. At Bronkhorst Spruit (Afrikaner for "watercress ditch"), the Boer commander informed them that the Boers had declared their independence. He warned them to turn back.

The British commander ordered his men to attack. The Boers, seeking cover behind trees and rocks, opened fire on the exposed British forces. Within minutes a third of the British soldiers were dead. Another third lay severely wounded. In a single encounter the Boers had eliminated an eighth of the British troops in the Transvaal.

At first the British government in London didn't pay much attention to the fighting in the Transvaal. They were preoccupied with Irish Nationalists, a problem much older and closer to home. But by February 1881 the Boers had Prime Minister

Fortification at Majuba Hill, Transvaal, 1890 *In 1877 the Boer state of Transvaal, or the South African Republic, was annexed by Great Britain. Three years later the Boers revolted and proclaimed a new Transvaal republic. They inflicted several stinging defeats on British forces sent against them, including an overwhelming one at Majuba Hill (February 27, 1881). These victories gave Paul Kruger (1828–1904) the leverage he needed to negotiate an end to the fighting and gave the Afrikaners limited independence. Because of these and other accomplishments, he became known as the builder of the Afrikaner nation.*

Gladstone's full attention. They continued to beat the British. In each instance small Boer forces repulsed larger groups of British soldiers and inflicted heavy losses. Sir Hercules Robinson, the new governor of the Cape Colony, ominously reported that Boers all over southern Africa were rising up against the British.

Prime Minister Gladstone realized he was facing another situation like the one in Ireland, where a British minority was trying to impose its will on a majority population that hated them. To avoid more bloodshed, he offered the Boers independence, with one condition: that the British would supervise their foreign relations.

On February 16, 1881, General Colley received formal instructions to offer peace and independence to the Boers. He felt humiliated at making "peace under defeat." The general wanted another chance to defeat the Boers and so redeem the honor of the British army. Colley relayed the peace offer but added his own conditions, which sabotaged the armistice and guaranteed at least one more battle. He insisted that Boer leader Paul Kruger respond within 48 hours, knowing that the message would not even reach Kruger in that time.

As the deadline passed, General Colley took up a position on a 2,000-foot-high table mountain, which commanded the country for miles around. Below him lay an important Boer military position. Colley saw no need to dig trenches because he believed his position was impregnable.

When the sun rose on the morning of February 27, 1881, and revealed the British on Majuba Hill, the Boers were left with a choice: dislodge the British from the high ground or surrender. Those who talked of retreat were labeled cowards. Up the rocky terrain went the unseen Boers, dressed in their everyday clothes, some hardly more than 13 or 14 years old. Each one, however, carried a modern rifle and knew how to use it with deadly efficiency. They overran the British position. Colley was among the 96 British soldiers killed in the attack. The loss of life became even more tragic when it was learned that Paul Kruger had accepted the peace offer.

The news of the defeat at Majuba Hill sent a shudder of humiliation through England. On March 23, 1881, the British and the Boers signed provisional peace terms. Later that summer the Pretoria Convention formally defined relations between Great Britain and the Transvaal, based on limited independence. The war was over. Even in defeat, however, the British presence in southern Africa stood strong. The British remained determined to protect their interests from other European nations. The dream of Lord Carnarvon and others for a larger empire had not ended.

Tswana Women Hairdressing, c. 1920

2

VISIONS OF GREATNESS

E nglish politicians weren't the only people who had plans for southern Africa. Perhaps the man with the biggest dreams of what he could gain from the vast territory was Cecil Rhodes. When Rhodes died in 1902, at the age of 48, he had become one of the most influential men in the world.

CECIL RHODES'S EARLY YEARS

Rhodes had always been ambitious. Born in England in 1853, he had planned on becoming either a clergyman, like his father, or a lawyer. Poor health kept him from going away to school as a young boy. His health did not improve as he grew older, so any path to the professions that had first intrigued him was effectively blocked. A congenital heart defect was probably the root cause of his many illnesses. It was also the reason he left England in 1870, at the age of 17, to find relief from his physical misery and weakness in the drier climate of southern Africa. He hoped to join his brother Herbert, who owned a cotton farm in Natal.

When he arrived Cecil Rhodes discovered that the farm was in financial trouble. Hoping to find a new source of income, his brother had traveled hundreds of miles across southern Africa to Griqualand West, where diamonds had been discovered three

Diamond Works, Vaal River, c. 1890 *Diamonds were discovered along the Vaal, Orange, and Harts Rivers in 1867. Three years later richer finds were made and a large-scale rush followed. Initially, individual diggers, both black and white, worked small claims by hand or using primitive machinery. The discovery of diamonds heightened British interest in gaining complete control of the Transvaal area.*

years earlier. Herbert Rhodes stayed long enough to stake a diamond claim near a promising hill named Colesberg Kopje. Then he came back, and the brothers spent a year trying to make the cotton farm profitable. In 1871 they returned to the diamond fields. Soon Cecil Rhodes was caught up in the diamond fever sweeping southern Africa. Within a decade he became one of the wealthiest men in the world.

The diamond rush in southern Africa began in 1867 when an African shepherd boy picked up a glittering piece of rock on some farmland near the Orange River. He traded it to an Afrikaner settler for several sheep, oxen, and a horse. The stone weighed 84 karats. As news of this discovery spread, both European and African diggers of all races swarmed to the area. The search for the stones first centered on the gravel beds of the Orange and Vaal Rivers and their tributaries. Three years later diggers began to find diamonds in the "blue ground" of certain volcanic formations. One of the richest sites uncovered was at Colesberg Kopje.

Despite the harsh conditions in the diamond camps, thousands of hopeful workers, and thousands more of those who had something to sell to them, poured into the area. The many camps around Colesberg Kopje grew into a town, which was named Kimberley in honor of British Colonial Secretary John Wodehouse, First Earl of Kimberley.

After working his diamond claim for two years, Herbert Rhodes gave up, but Cecil persisted. He looked much too young and frail to survive such a brutal environment, but this shy young man had big dreams. When he described his vision of European expansion into the interior of Africa, men applauded him. Though he was an extremely nervous person and ill at ease in most groups, his personal charisma inspired loyalty and devotion among friends and business associates.

During the 1870s Cecil Rhodes split his time between Kimberley and England, where he attended Oxford University.

At Oxford Rhodes put more effort into student pranks than into the work required for degrees in Latin and ancient history. He often told stories about sneaking off to the horse races without being caught by his teachers. Rhodes's eccentricities—his obsession with wealth, his commitment to imperialism, even his fascination with his own death—intrigued his fellow students. He enjoyed polo and other competitive games, but it was clear that amassing a fortune in Africa was likely to be his greatest victory.

THE DE BEERS DIAMOND MINE

Rhodes established himself in the diamond industry by purchasing a claim to the De Beers mine in 1871. While in England, Rhodes sent detailed instructions for managing the mine to his De Beers business partners. His persistence paid off. At first simply one of many speculative diggers, Rhodes eventually became recognized as the most successful diamond miner with a brilliant mind for business. He saw the diamond industry as a foundation for personal wealth and believed the best way to develop this wealth was to consolidate ownership of the diamond mines.

In the 1870s, working with his lifelong friend Charles D. Rudd, Rhodes purchased other diamond mines. The two men formed the De Beers Mining Company, which still operates. Although Rudd didn't have Rhodes's business skills, he was completely trustworthy, a quality Rhodes valued immensely. It was Rudd's trustworthiness that allowed Rhodes to spend the better part of eight years studying at Oxford.

RHODES'S ENTRANCE INTO POLITICS

Rhodes's vision included more than simply accumulating enormous wealth. He wanted to build a railway from the Cape of Good Hope to Cairo. He also dreamed of uniting the Boers and the British in southern Africa, as part of the British Empire. To achieve these lofty dreams, he realized he had to be involved in politics. In 1881, having completed his studies at Oxford and settled back in Kimberley, Rhodes was elected to the Cape Colony parliament. His constituency included many Boers, who respected him for his challenging ideas. Although he stumbled awkwardly through his speeches, the individual conversations that followed were always compelling. Whoever he was talking to and whatever he had to say, Cecil Rhodes never forgot his vision for expanding British interests north toward the interior of Africa.

This obsession involved him in several important decisions concerning land claims in southern Africa during the

Khoikhoi People, c. 1920 *The first European explorers found the Khoikhoi living in the remote interior of South Africa. War, disease, and absorption into other neighboring communities have dissipated most of the original Khoikhoi. Their traditional economy and social organization have changed dramatically; most have become Christians and have adopted the dress, language, and general mode of living in a Europeanized rural environment.*

1880s. The first situation arose in 1882. Discontent in Basutoland—present-day Lesotho—had to be addressed. The Sotho were a proud African people with strong national traditions and a history of maintaining their independence against Zulu, Boer, and British threats. Rhodes served on a commission appointed to settle conflicting claims. There he met General Charles Gordon, the former British governor of the Egyptian Sudan. Gordon organized meetings with the African chiefs involved in the conflict. Through discussion rather than force, the conflict was resolved. Rhodes was most impressed by Gordon's handling of what seemed to be an intractable situation.

CONTROL OF BECHUANALAND

That same year Rhodes began pushing for Cape Colony control of Bechuanaland, west of the Cape Colony—now Lesotho and Botswana. He saw it as a corridor for expanding British influence toward the interior of Africa, giving greater access to new mineral riches. Thomas Scanlen, the prime minister of the Cape, saw things differently. To him Bechuanaland was a useless desert expanse full of fighting African tribes. He wanted nothing to do with it. Besides, the rebellion in Basutoland and construction of new railroads had already placed the Cape too far in debt. Prime Minister Scanlen didn't want to spend any money to expand the Cape's frontiers.

Frustrated, Rhodes turned to London. He warned that settlers from the Transvaal were claiming land in Bechuanaland and trying to establish several independent Boer republics. If they weren't stopped, Rhodes feared the entire area would be claimed by the Transvaal Boers who, along with the Germans in South West Africa, would then cut off the Cape Colony from any access to the north.

At first the British government was unconvinced, but in 1884 Prime Minister Gladstone's government changed its position. In part it was persuaded by Hercules Robinson, British high commissioner at the Cape, who passed on Rhodes's arguments in a more polished form. In February 1884 Paul Kruger, now president of the Transvaal, arrived in London to rework parts of the Pretoria Convention (1881). In exchange for almost complete Boer control over internal affairs in the Transvaal and a British promise to stop protecting African rights within the region, Kruger accepted a western boundary for the Transvaal that excluded any part of Bechuanaland.

John Mackenzie, a well-known British missionary, was appointed deputy commissioner of the new Bechuanaland protectorate in 1884. Because Mackenzie championed the rights of Africans who lived in Bechuanaland, he antagonized the resident Boers. Mackenzie emphatically declared that the British would protect Africans in his territory from Boer mistreatment. Rhodes felt it was critical to regain Boer trust if there was ever to be any hope of a unified white community under the British flag in southern Africa. He insisted that Mackenzie be fired and that Rhodes himself be appointed deputy commissioner in his place.

After his appointment, however, Cecil Rhodes found that he had underestimated Paul Kruger. The president of the Transvaal worked behind the scenes to convince the Boers in Bechuanaland to stay loyal to the Transvaal. Nothing Cecil Rhodes promised the Bechuanaland Boers could break the grip of their solidarity with the Transvaal.

When the government in London learned of the growing tensions between the Africans, the Boers, and the British, they sent Charles Warren, along with 5,000 British troops, to restore order to the region. In 1885 the British sponsored a conference near the Vaal River. Both Rhodes and Kruger attended. When the meeting was over, Kruger surrendered all claim to Bechuanaland, and the territory was divided into northern and southern sections. Southern Bechuanaland became a crown colony, and Northern Bechuanaland became a British protectorate.

Rhodes, who wanted all the territory annexed to the Cape Colony, showed his disagreement with the decision by resigning as deputy commissioner. The news wasn't all bad for Rhodes, however. His fear of the Transvaal Boers' taking over Bechuanaland was settled, and this agreement laid the foundation for his dream of a northern railway route to the interior of Africa.

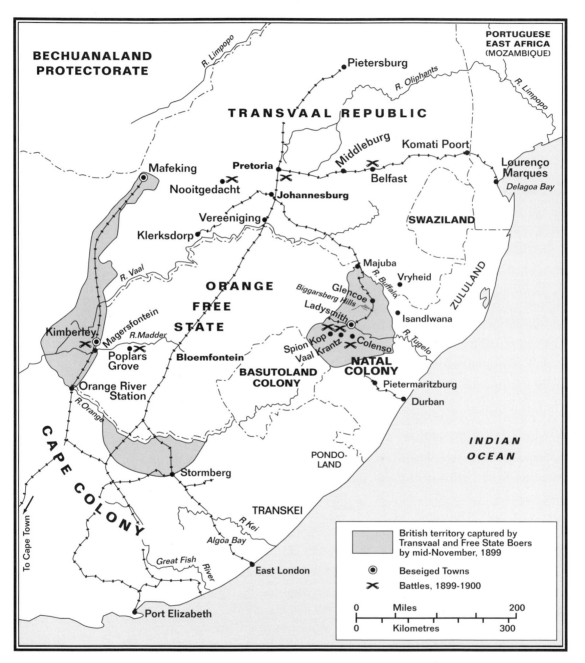

South Africa: The South African War, 1899–1902

Map labels:

BECHUANALAND PROTECTORATE

PORTUGUESE EAST AFRICA (MOZAMBIQUE)

R. Limpopo

Pietersburg

R. Oliphants

R. Limpopo

TRANSVAAL REPUBLIC

Middleburg

Komati Poort

Mafeking

Pretoria

Nooitgedacht

Belfast

Lourenço Marques

Delagoa Bay

Johannesburg

SWAZILAND

Vereeniging

Klerksdorp

Majuba

Vryheid

R. Vaal

ORANGE

Biggarsberg Hills

Glencoe

R. Buffalo

FREE

Ladysmith

Isandlwana

STATE

ZULULAND

Kimberley

Magersfontein

R. Madder

Spion Kop

Vaal Krantz

Colenso

Poplars Grove

Bloemfontein

NATAL COLONY

R. Tugelo

Orange River Station

BASUTOLAND COLONY

Pietermaritzburg

R. Orange

Durban

CAPE COLONY

INDIAN OCEAN

Stormberg

PONDO-LAND

To Cape Town

TRANSKEI

R. Kei

Algoa Bay

Great Fish River

East London

Port Elizabeth

Legend:

British territory captured by Transvaal and Free State Boers by mid-November, 1899

Beseiged Towns

Battles, 1899-1900

0   Miles   200

0   Kilometres   300

THE KIMBERLEY MINE

Rhodes remained a member of the Cape Colony parliament, and his political and business accomplishments attracted both new friends and powerful rivals. One of the most important partnerships Cecil Rhodes ever formed was with Alfred Beit, a German. Beit had an unequaled knowledge both of diamond mining and of how to raise the vast sums of money necessary to support a rapidly expanding business. In many ways Beit and Rhodes were opposites. Beit hated any publicity and was perfectly happy to let Rhodes stand in the limelight. Beit's knowledge of financing helped Rhodes bring his dreams to life. Working with Beit, Rhodes bought out many more diamond claims. Eventually he controlled all the mines in the original De Beers claim.

Rhodes was not satisfied to simply own all the De Beers mines. He next set his sights on the famed Kimberley mine. This mine was largely controlled by Barney Barnato, who headed the Barnato Diamond Mining Company. Barnato wanted to control the diamond industry just as much as did Rhodes. He was the son of a Jewish shopkeeper, had grown up in the rough East End of London, and had traveled with his brother to Africa in 1873 when they learned of the diamond rush. The two men established a diamond brokerage firm the next year. Then Barney Barnato bought up many diamond claims, hoping that some of them would be very valuable. His speculative investment paid off, and in 1880 he formed the Barnato Diamond Mining Company. Barney Barnato soon controlled more of the diamond industry than anyone other than Cecil Rhodes.

Beginning in 1887, Cecil Rhodes bought all the diamond shares he could get his hands on. Barnato did the same. Clearly only one company could control the diamond industry of southern Africa. By 1888 Rhodes had won the battle. He incorporated all his diamond mines under the De Beers Consolidated Mines, Ltd., and bought out Barney Barnato with a $25 million (almost $450 million today) settlement. Not one to hold a grudge, Rhodes also made his former business adversary a governor for life in the company.

Mining Machinery, Witwatersrand District, Transvaal, 1890 *In 1886 prospectors determined that a 40-mile belt of gold-bearing ore encircled what is the present-day city of Johannesburg. The rapid growth of the gold-mining industry intensified the Europeanization processes started by the diamond boom (1867)—namely, urbanization, capital investment, infrastructural development, and the growth of a laboring class. By 1899 gold mining employed (or exploited) about 109,000 people, of whom some 97,000 were African workers. Today, four countries—South Africa, Russia, the United States, and Australia—account for two-thirds of the gold produced annually throughout the world. South Africa alone, with its vast Witwatersrand district, produces about one-third of the world's gold.*

GOLD MINING

Diamonds were not the only valuable product to be found in southern Africa. Gold was discovered in the Transvaal, and in 1886 Cecil Rhodes made his second fortune by investing cautiously in the new gold mines. All the activity was centered in the Witwatersrand (Afrikaner for "ridge of white waters"). The ridge lay between the Vaal and Limpopo Rivers, well over 200 miles northeast of the Kimberley diamond mines.

Unlike most other gold discoveries around the world during the 1800s, the ore found in the Witwatersrand (or the Rand, as it came to be called) could be extracted economically only by using complex machinery. This meant that independent miners couldn't afford to excavate the gold. The only people financially capable of extracting the great wealth hidden in the Rand were the biggest diamond financiers. By the end of 1886, the Rand had been divided between Cecil Rhodes, Alfred Beit, Julius Wernher, Barney Barnato, and J. B. Robinson. Many English and German diggers descended on the area. The Boer government of the Transvaal sent two men to choose a site that would be suitable for a city. The city was named Johannesburg, and within 10 years it grew to 100,000 people.

By 1888 Cecil Rhodes was extremely wealthy. Through his ownership of both diamond and gold mines, he had made his fortune several times over. But he never forgot his vision of uniting the whites of southern Africa and pushing its territories north. After his experiences with Bechuanaland at the beginning of the decade, Rhodes didn't trust either the Cape Colony or the British government to take appropriate action.

The British South Africa Company (BSAC)

In his view the Cape Colony leadership had a limited vision and the British government was too easily influenced by missionaries who fought continuously for the rights of Africans. Rhodes decided on a different course. He created a public company that operated under a royal charter. Its purpose was to acquire and exercise commercial and administrative rights in south central Africa.

The British South Africa Company (BSAC) was incorporated in 1889. Significantly, the charter placed no northern limit on the territory that the BSAC could control. Cecil

Camping, Witwatersrand District, Transvaal, 1890 *In 1886 gold was discovered in the Boer-controlled Transvaal. A major gold rush began, which resulted in an influx of primarily English-speaking miners and fortune seekers who were called Uitlanders by the Boers. The Boers, or Afrikaners, afraid of being overwhelmed by the Uitlanders, passed laws to strengthen their control—such as the 1888 law that made Dutch the only language to be used in legal proceedings and official documents. British support for the Uitlanders finally erupted into the South African, or Boer, War (1898–1902).*

Unlike the goldfields of North America and Australia, which petered out after a few years of being worked, the Witwatersrand (or the Rand) mining operations continued to grow and are now the world's largest producers of gold. Also, the geology of the Witwatersrand necessitated large machinery for extracting the gold-bearing ore from the earth. Therefore, small independent miners, so common in other gold rushes, were either bought out or forced out by large mining corporations.

Rhodes was elated. He was in a perfect position to achieve his goals of obtaining mineral wealth, building railroads, and encouraging white settlement in the northern reaches of southern Africa.

Rhodes often remarked: "It is no use having big ideas if you have not the cash to carry them out." He had both.

Church of England Mission, Near Mafeking, c. 1920 *From the time of the Reformation in the 16th century, the Church of England expanded by following the routes of British exploration and colonization. Vigorous missionary work occurred in South Africa. The church has left an impressive legacy of educational and medical facilities. In modern times the church actively opposed the South African government's policy of apartheid (enforced separation for whites and blacks) until that policy was abolished.*

3

PEOPLE ON
A MISSION

Entrepreneurs like Cecil Rhodes were not the first white people with a vision for carving a path to the center of Africa. Long before Rhodes was born, others were arriving in southern Africa to spread the three Cs: Christianity, civilization, and commerce.

ROBERT MOFFAT

Most Europeans did not acknowledge that cultures different from their own were civilized. When missionaries first encountered the vast differences in political organization, economic structure, and social customs between their culture and that of the Africans, they were both fascinated and shocked.

Though they were idealistic and well-intentioned, the missionaries were also British. They could not avoid the conclusion that these "tribal people" needed more than conversion to Christianity in order to survive. They believed that the Africans also needed to be "uplifted" and "civilized" through contact with European culture, much of which they thought was an authentic expression of Christianity. The missionaries saw conversion to

Christianity as just the first step in a long and difficult process of social transformation for Africans.

The missionaries were particularly appalled by the slave trade in Africa. Although slavery had been outlawed in Britain and the importation of slaves was illegal in the United States, an active slave trade continued between Africa and the Arab nations. The missionaries wanted to create other commercial ventures so that Africans could make a living without being dependent on this odious system.

Robert Moffat of Scotland arrived in southern Africa in 1816. He was 20 years old. Sent by the London Missionary Society, he spent seven years moving from place to place and learning a great deal about the people who lived in the region. War among the Zulus often forced him to relocate. Finally, Robert Moffat settled at Kuruman, about 600 miles north of Cape Town on the southeastern edge of the Kalahari Desert. He lived there with his wife and children for 49 years.

As Moffat traveled throughout southeastern Africa, he learned the Tswana language and created an alphabet for it. This task was difficult because like many other African languages, Tswana included clicking sounds that did not exist in European languages. In 1830 he published his Tswana translation of the Gospel of Luke. Over the next three decades, he finished a Tswana translation of the entire Bible, as well as *A Book of Hymns in Chuana* and a translation of *Pilgrim's Progress* by John Bunyan. His work helped preserve the Tswana language, and his writings describing the people he encountered left a record of the Tswana civilization before it was changed by European influence.

Moffat also introduced different methods of farming and irrigation which improved crop production. He built a dam at Kuruman and planted an orchard. The mission station flourished. Like other mission stations in southern Africa, Kuruman became a home for African peasant farmers, who raised enough food to provide for their families. This situation was much

Sable Antelope, Botswana, c. 1910 *Pictured here is Chauncy Stigand's guide standing behind a sable antelope. Stigand— (1877–1919), British military officer, explorer, geographer, and game hunter—was a swashbuckling adventurer who projected courage and zeal in his exploits throughout the British Empire. He was a heroic figure upon whom the British heaped adulation. Stigand's articles about hunting in Africa appeared in popular magazines. He recounted how he had been "tossed and gored by a rhinoceros, mauled by a lion, and almost trampled to death by a wounded elephant."*

The sable antelope lives in herds in the forests of southern Africa. Like the related roan antelope, the sable is a graceful animal with an erect mane, long hair on the throat, and parallel sickle-shaped horns. It stands just less than five feet at the shoulder.

better than the situation Africans found in most areas settled by whites. There they were usually forced to become slaves or indentured servants. At Kuruman both African boys and girls were offered a Western-style education. Many of the African people Moffat met converted to Christianity.

DAVID LIVINGSTONE

In 1840 Robert Moffat met David Livingstone. He recognized Livingstone's talents and encouraged him to become a missionary in Africa. Livingstone had grown up in a one-room tenement near Glasgow, Scotland, with his parents, two brothers, and two sisters. When he turned 10, he went to work 14 hours a day in a cotton mill. After work he attended classes for another two hours.

David Livingstone loved learning so much that he spent the first money he earned on a Latin grammar book. He took the book to work and propped it up against one of the machines. Each time he walked by the machine, he read a line from the book. Eventually he learned both Latin and Greek in this way. Then he read the works of Virgil and Horace in their original languages as well as many theological books.

Livingstone loved science and wanted to become a medical doctor. His father, however, would approve of such training only if it were for a religious purpose. Thus young Livingstone decided to become a medical missionary to China. The remarkable success of his self-tutoring in foreign languages, theology, and science earned Livingstone, at the age of 23, a place at Anderson's College in Glasgow. He rapidly expanded his previous areas of knowledge and also studied medicine. A year later, when he was ready to apply to be a missionary doctor to China, the Opium Wars in that country made it impossible for him to go. So Livingstone set his sights on Africa. He landed in Cape Town on March 14, 1841.

Livingstone loved adventure. He traveled to places in Africa that no European had ever seen before, including Victoria Falls,

Tswana Women, 1908 *The Tswana lived in what the Europeans called Bechuanaland, the present area of Botswana. The Tswana traditionally are farmers. They are part of the Sotho, a Bantu-speaking people of South Africa. Today, there is a seasonal migration of large numbers of Tswana men who work in the mines and industrial centers of South Africa.*

which he named for Britain's queen. In 1844 he visited the village of Mabotsa near the Kuruman station.

While there, he learned that lions were killing many of the villagers' cattle. Livingstone persuaded the villagers to join him in hunting the lions. When they discovered a pride of lions resting on a rock, he took careful aim at the largest male and fired with both barrels of his shotgun.

The wounded beast attacked Livingstone while the missionary was trying to reload, sinking its teeth into Livingstone's left arm and shaking him wildly. An elderly man from the village named Mebalwe grabbed another rifle and shot at the lion. The lion dropped Livingstone and fastened its jaws on Mebalwe's thigh. Finally, it tossed him aside and pounced on still another villager, only to drop dead in mid-attack.

The bone of Livingstone's arm was shattered. He reset the bone himself but ultimately lost the use of that arm. He stayed with the Moffats at Kuruman while he was healing from his injuries and subsequently proposed to their daughter Mary. She accepted.

Robert Moffat was an unusual missionary in the 19th century because he spent most of his time at Kuruman. Missionaries, merchants, and others with business abroad during that century typically were separated from their families for months and sometimes years at a time.

For the first seven years of their marriage, Mary Moffat Livingstone tried to follow the pattern of living she had experienced in her parents' household. She was used to the hardships of life near the desert, so she often traveled with her new husband. In 1849 Livingstone and his team became the first Europeans to reach Lake Nagami on the northern edge of the Kalahari Desert

Servants, Okavango River, c. 1910 *These servants accompanied Chauncy Stigand on his Okavango River hunting expedition, c. 1910. Stigand was one of a band of Englishmen for whom a distant frontier posed the challenge of an adventure. Among his most popular books were:* Black Tales for White Children *and* Tropical Cookery.

and to leave a written record of their journey. This earned him a gold medal from the Royal Geographical Society.

David Livingstone's goal to open a "missionary road," 1,500 miles north into the interior of Africa, strained his wife's abilities. She was responsible not only for herself, but also for their young children. When their newborn baby died after they wandered through the desert for a month with limited water supplies, the Livingstones decided that it was too difficult for their young family to travel as part of an expedition. Mary and the children took a ship from Cape Town and returned to Britain. David Livingstone continued exploring southern Africa and spreading Christianity. They did not see each other again for four years.

Biographers argue over which passion was most important to Livingstone: the desire to explore Africa and extend the borders of the British Empire, the desire to end slavery, or the desire to spread Christianity. Some argue that his actual impact on the slave trade was minimal. Effective or not, his active support for treating Africans with dignity and preserving their rights angered the white Afrikaners who depended on slaves to make their farms profitable. The Afrikaners burned his mission station and stole his animals, hoping to drive him away. Livingstone's conflicts with whites were not limited to Afrikaners. He fought with other missionaries, fellow explorers, and even his own assistants, especially when these people disagreed with his views of how Africans should be treated.

Most missionaries had a paternalistic attitude toward Africans, treating them as children who needed guidance from more sophisticated white people. Although David Livingstone could not entirely avoid the paternalism of his British background, he also treated Africans with respect. In response to those who claimed that African people were impossible to understand or get along with he said, "Africans are not by any means unreasonable. I think unreasonableness is more a heredity disease in Europe."

Livingstone returned to England in 1856 and was reunited with his family. While there, he wrote a 400-page book called *Missionary Travels and Researches in South Africa.* It remains an indispensable source about the precolonial history of Africa. From the moment of its release, it was also a best-seller, with more than 70,000 copies sold. People were enthralled with his tales of adventure, and they responded with outrage to his stories of the continuing horrors of slavery. Livingstone's book further encouraged explorers and merchants to perceive southern Africa as a land full of economic opportunity.

Proceeds from the sale of the book earned Livingstone more than 120 times his usual salary from the London Missionary Society (LMS). This money helped him rescue his family from poverty and gave him financial security at a time when he was increasingly at odds with his employers. The LMS wanted him to be a more traditional missionary and not put so much energy into exploration. Livingstone, on the other hand, saw his work as "missionary travels." He argued that he was preparing God's highway for those who followed. By the time Livingstone and his family departed England in the spring of 1858, he and the LMS had parted ways.

Mary Livingstone once again traveled with her husband as he explored the Zambezi River. This trip was a disaster from the beginning. Their boat leaked so badly that they had to abandon it, and other equipment proved to be useless as well. Many members of the expedition died from malaria and other diseases. In 1862, shortly after giving birth to her sixth child, Mary also died.

Two years later David Livingstone took one last trip back to England. While there, he published his book *Narrative of an Expedition to the Zambezi and Its Tributaries.* Once again, the public was captivated by the dangerous exploits Livingstone described. With financing from the Royal Geographical Society and wealthy friends, David Livingstone headed back to Africa with the twin goals of finding the source of the Nile

River and exposing the continuing slave trade. He missed finding the source of the Nile by about 200 miles, and his death in 1873 came a month before the British closed the largest slave market on the east coast of Africa.

THE INFLUENCE OF THE MISSIONARIES

Within 10 years the southern Africa known by David Livingstone and his father-in-law, Robert Moffat, had largely disappeared. Independent African nations were falling under British control. With increasing frequency, missionaries were used by both Africans and the British as translators and intermediaries.

In some cases, such as that of John Mackenzie, who was displaced by Cecil Rhodes as deputy commissioner of Bechuanaland, they used their influence to champion African rights. Others betrayed Africans to help the British gain control of valuable land and mineral rights. One of the worst examples of those who betrayed Africans was Charles Helm of the London Missionary Society. In 1888 Helm purposely mistranslated a crucial document from partners working with Cecil Rhodes and thereby cheated Lobengula, the Ndebele king, out of his land.

Christian teachings about the equality and dignity of each individual greatly reduced the slave trade. At the same time missionary condemnation of African customs and institutions damaged traditional social structures by diminishing the chief's authority in many groups.

Many missionaries also encouraged Africans to participate in the developing colonial labor market. Such work usually required young men to be absent from their families for months at a time. Although the missionaries may have done this with the hope that it would bring economic security during a time of great change, it actually encouraged the further breakdown of African society.

Missionary schools educated generations of African children and helped them to understand the forces that were changing their world. From this pool of educated Christian Africans would rise up outspoken critics of colonialism who would be catalysts for returning respect and power to black people in southern Africa.

Market Street, Johannesburg, c. 1925 *Founded in 1886 following the discovery of gold, Johannesburg, within 40 years, had become the world's largest city not on a navigable body of water. It was laid out in a rectangular grid pattern that is unchanged from the first 1886 survey. By the 1920's, monumental Beaux Arts structures had replaced the tents and clay huts of the original mining camps. Also, by the 1920's, racial segregation had made Johannesburg the capital of urban apartheid. These discriminatory laws were repealed in 1991. Today, about 75 percent of the city's citizens are Africans but the city still retains a high degree of racial separation with a majority of Africans living in "townships" on the urban periphery.*

4

CAUGHT IN THE MIDDLE

Beginning with the Dutch and Portuguese, Europeans had been arriving in southern Africa since the 1500s. They usually stayed close to the coast and were primarily interested in trade. The Europeans had sporadic contact with groups of African hunters and herdsmen from further inland but they knew little about these people and how they lived. The Africans spoke a variety of languages, which the Europeans found difficult to master. Instead, they expected the people with whom they traded ivory, metal, and other products to learn their European languages.

The hunter groups scattered throughout southern Africa had adapted their lifestyles to fit the terrain where they lived. Some specialized in pursuing animals and gathering plants near the Kalahari Desert. Others lived in the mountains. A third type of hunter lived in well-watered country with abundant supplies of game. All of the hunters ate fruits and fresh and dried meat. They brought down individual animals with poisoned arrows and trapped large herds in pits concealed in the ground.

THE KHOIKHOI
The Khoikhoi, one of the largest groups of herders, lived a nomadic life, traveling from one grazing area to another with large numbers of sheep and cattle. A camp of

Village Along the Okavango River, c. 1910 *Chauncy Hugh Stigand was indefatigable in compiling notes on the manners and customs of the various tribes with whom he came in contact. His photographs are an important part of the Royal Geographical Society's collection on South Africa. Stigand attempted to write down phonetically the speech patterns of the various peoples he encountered on his numerous trips throughout Africa. At one point, he spent more than a year living on Lamu Island off the East Africa coast to compile a vocabulary of the dialect spoken there.*

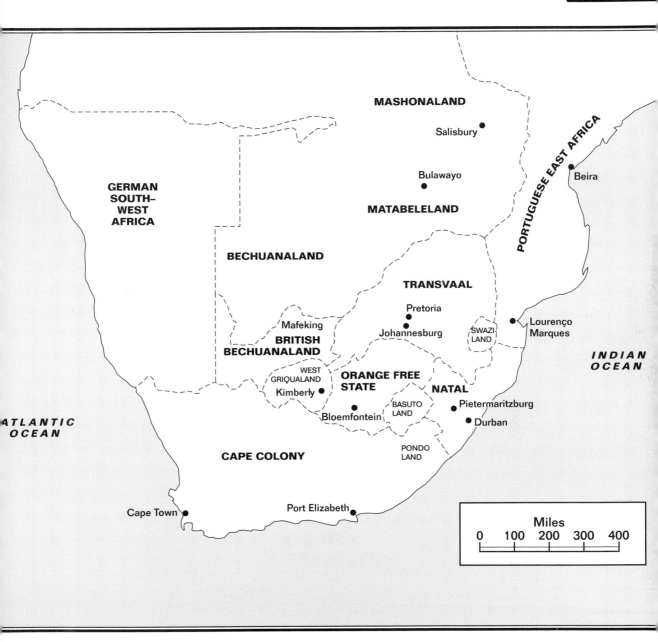

MASHONALAND

Salisbury

Bulawayo

MATABELELAND

PORTUGUESE EAST AFRICA

Beira

GERMAN SOUTH–WEST AFRICA

BECHUANALAND

TRANSVAAL

Pretoria

Johannesburg

Mafeking

BRITISH BECHUANALAND

SWAZILAND

Lourenço Marques

INDIAN OCEAN

WEST GRIQUALAND

ORANGE FREE STATE

Kimberly

NATAL

Pietermaritzburg

BASUTO LAND

Bloemfontein

Durban

ATLANTIC OCEAN

CAPE COLONY

PONDO LAND

Cape Town

Port Elizabeth

Miles

0 100 200 300 400

Southern Africa c. 1890

250 men, women, and children might have 1,500 or 1,600 cattle. Their diet included milk, meat, fish, and honey, which they used to brew mead. They used the oxen in the herds as pack animals when they moved their camps one area to another. The Khoikhoi also rode their oxen and controlled the ox's movement by means of a bridle made from a stick fastened through the animal's nose cartilage.

Chiefdoms were made up of groups of farmers who controlled areas with good soil and growing conditions. These chiefdoms were quite flexible. They intermingled with groups of hunters and herdsmen. When a group within the chiefdom disagreed with its leaders, they simply left and formed another chiefdom. War rarely took place. Although each group spoke its own language, the languages were similar enough so that people could communicate with each other easily and even move from one group to another.

This situation changed near the end of the 18th century and in early part of the 19th century. One factor was that the amount of farmland was limited, and the various groups had occupied just about all of the land that could be farmed. Resolving disputes by picking up and moving to another location was no longer an option.

Also, the relationship between Europeans and Africans was changing. European settlements were expanding, and people interested in farming the land and raising livestock wanted to move away from port areas such as Cape Town. Europeans did not understand that Africans frequently shared land, rather than owning it. When Europeans found an area that suited their needs, they simply drove the Africans away. Often, the same people who had previously farmed the land or grazed their herds on it were forced to work for the Europeans as either slaves or servants. Many Africans lost their lives to diseases such as smallpox, measles, and influenza, which were introduced by Europeans.

THE GRIQUA

The Dutch in the Cape Colony and the Khoikhoi had traded with each other with few problems during most of the 1700s. In some cases the Dutch and the Khoikhoi had mixed offspring who were largely Christian and spoke Afrikaans. These people became known as Griqua, named after an ancestor whom many of them held in common. The Dutch refused to grant citizenship rights such as land ownership to the Griquas. This made it impossible for the Griqua to make a living without becoming virtual slaves. Thus late in the 18th century, many of them fled to Griqualand, located northwest of the juncture of the Vaal and Orange Rivers, the present southwestern KwaZulu/Natal Province.

Those who stayed in the Cape Colony became translators and farmworkers. Although they were theoretically free, they could do nothing to protect themselves if their masters treated them like slaves. Slaves had no control over what happened to their children and were not allowed to possess weapons. If a master killed a slave, he was not punished if he could establish that it had not been his intent to kill. Among the Khoikhoi and Griqua, the deathrate was high and the birthrate was low.

The Griqua who fled to Griqualand were joined by missionaries in 1802. In the 1820s they successfully defended themselves against invaders during the *Difaqane,* a Sesotho word meaning "forced migration," or "the time of troubles." The *Difaqane* was a time when African groups, fleeing Zulu warriors to the southeast, displaced many of the people who already lived between the Drakensberg Mountains, the Kalahari Desert, and the Limpopo River. The Zulu word for this time is the *Mfecane*, meaning "the crushing."

During this decade the Griquas split into two communities. One group, led by Adries Waterboer, remained in Griqua Town and became known as the West Griqua. The other group, led by Adam Kok II, moved to Philippolis and became known as the East Griqua. Missionaries from the London Missionary Society worked with both groups of Griquas and tried to convince them that they should become settled farmers with Western-style political institutions.

Change continued in the 1830s when Boers left the Cape Colony to escape British rule and establish an independent land for themselves. Many of them settled around Philippolis. They rented land from the East Griquas for small amounts of money. They ignored Adam Kok's authority and encroached on land owned by both East Griquas and southern Sothos, another African group in the area.

John Philip, the South African superintendent of the London Missionary Society, tried to convince British authorities that, for both humanitarian and practical reasons, it was in their interest to protect the Africans. Treaties were made that guaranteed British protection of the East Griquas, but the financial resources to support this protection never materialized. By 1854 all treaties between the East Griquas and Britain had been negated. The Griquas, other African groups, and the Boers were left to work things out among themselves. Realizing that his people would inevitably be forced to sell all their land, Adam Kok sold out his rights north of the Orange River to the Orange Free State. He then led his people across the Drakensberg, where they founded a new Griqualand East. There they lived peacefully until the 1870s, when white farmers once again appeared. By 1879 the Cape Colony annexed Griqualand East. As Kok had feared, most Griquas were forced to sell their land; and by the end of the 19th century, few Griquas remained in the land that bore their name.

After the *Difaqane* the West Griquas were mostly left alone. However, they still faced the widespread loss of livestock to disease, the destruction of many big game animals, and the effects of a long drought. Alcohol-related problems also developed when Cape traders introduced a cheap brandy called Cape Smoke. Nicholas Waterboer succeeded his father as chief in 1853, but he was unable to help his people overcome any of these crises. By 1870 the West Griqua population had declined to less than a thousand.

When diamonds were discovered in Griqualand West, both the Afrikaners and the British were ready to stake claims to the territory. The British summarily annexed Griqualand West. In 1875 the British government formed a land court to untangle

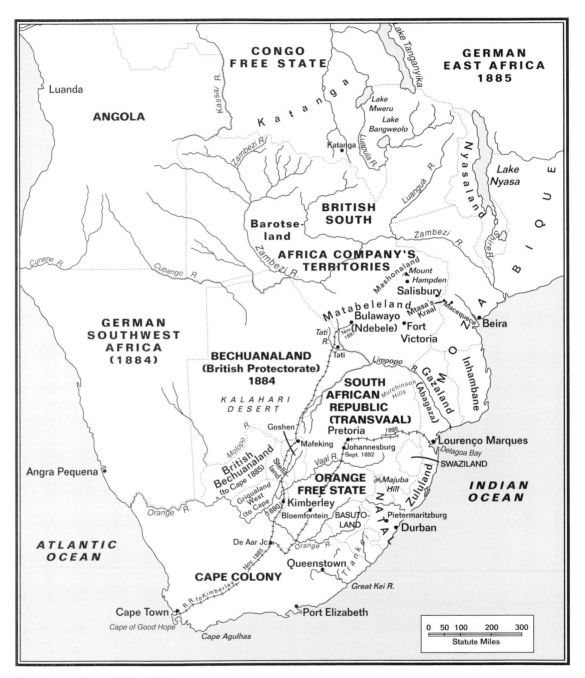

Southern Africa 1880–1900

Within the map:

CONGO
FREE STATE

GERMAN
EAST AFRICA
1885

Luanda

ANGOLA

Kassai R.

Zambezi R.

K a t a n g a

Lake
Mweru
Lake
Bangweolo

Katanga

Luapula R.

Luangua R.

Lake Tanganyika

Nyasaland

Lake
Nyasa

BRITISH
SOUTH

Barotse-
land

Zambezi R.

Cunene R.

Cubango R.

AFRICA COMPANY'S
TERRITORIES

Zambezi R.

Mashonaland

*Mount
Hampden*

Salisbury

M O Z A M B I Q U E

Shire R.

GERMAN
SOUTHWEST
AFRICA
(1884)

M a t a b e l e l a n d

Bulawayo
(Ndebele)

*Tati
R.*

Nov.1881

Tati

Fort
Victoria

Mtasa's
Kraal

Macequece

Beira

Inhambane

BECHUANALAND
(British Protectorate)
1884

*KALAHARI
DESERT*

Limpopo

R.

Gazaland
(Abagaza)

Goshen

Molopo R.

SOUTH
AFRICAN
REPUBLIC
(TRANSVAAL)

Pretoria

*Murchinson
Hills*

1895

Mafeking

Johannesburg
Sept. 1892

Lourenço Marques

Delagoa Bay

SWAZILAND

Angra Pequena

British
Bechuanaland
(to Cape 1885)

Stella
land

Vaal R.

ORANGE
FREE STATE

Majuba
Hill

Griqualand
West
(to Cape)

1880

Kimberley

Bloemfontein

BASUTO
LAND

Orange R.

N
A
T
A
L

Zululand

Pietermaritzburg

Durban

INDIAN
OCEAN

ATLANTIC
OCEAN

De Aar Jc.

Orange R.

Nov.1885

R.R. to Kimberley

CAPE COLONY

Queenstown

Transkei

Great Kei R.

Cape Town

Cape of Good Hope

Cape Agulhas

Port Elizabeth

0 50 100 200 300
Statute Miles

the conflicting claims to what had unexpectedly become valuable property. The court ruled that titles based on grants made by Waterboer were invalid and awarded a large cash compensation to the Orange Free State. The British also restricted licenses for dealing in diamonds to white people. The Griqua and other African inhabitants of the area committed sporadic acts of violence in protest. Volunteer white forces responded quickly and killed many Africans.

In 1880 Griqualand West become part of the Cape Colony. The Griquas were given farms, but they quickly sold the land to white people in exchange for either cash or liquor. By the end of the century, the Griqua no longer existed as a community. The few survivors worked for the whites who had taken possession of their land.

The Tswana

Another group of Africans who lived north of Griqualand West also faced changes because of the European presence during the 19th century. The Tswana people lived on territory that included the only road north of Kuruman that went deep into the interior of Africa. Both the British and Afrikaners were set on controlling this territory primarily because of that road. British control would guarantee missionaries and traders secure access to the far interior. Afrikaner control would allow the Transvaal to block the road, thereby eliminating British influence from its western border. Neither the British nor the Afrikaners were interested in dominating the Tswana people. They simply wanted to control the territory.

The Tswana were themselves deeply divided. The fierce rivalries between their many chiefdoms often led to war. Dynastic quarrels further weakened individual chiefdoms. Tswana leaders often supported either the British or the Afrikaners simply to strengthen their position within the group. Anarchy soon spread throughout the entire Tswana territory.

The Pretoria Convention (1881) between Britain and the Transvaal established a western boundary for the Afrikaners far

Tswana Fortune-Tellers, c. 1920 *Christianity brought by European missionaries became the official religion of the eight Tswana states by the end of the 19th century. Indigenous religious and medical practices, especially respect for patriarchal ancestors, were often blended together with popular Christian beliefs. Fortune-telling is not part of Christian theology, although it played an important part in most African religions.*

Tswana Rope Makers, c. 1910 *These Tswana men are combing out fibers and making rope from clumps of reeds growing in the immense Okavango Swamp in northern Botswana.*

short of the northern road. It also failed to resolve the conflicts in the Tswana territory. As Afrikaner farmers moved beyond the borders of the Transvaal, they made agreements with various chiefs and supported them in their conflicts. The British in Griqualand West became advisers to other chiefdoms. The rising tensions throughout the area gave the Transvaal an opportunity to create two independent republics within Griqualand West: Stellaland and Goshen. These republics blocked the road to the north, creating an unacceptable situation for the British.

In 1884 a new compromise agreement between the Afrikaners and the British adjusted the western boundary of the Transvaal. The British government asked missionary John Mackenzie to act as deputy commissioner for the territory. Mackenzie convinced some of the chiefdoms to accept British protection, but Cecil Rhodes then forced Mackenzie out and took over his position. Rhodes had no better success at controlling the Afrikaners in Goshen, and eventually the British sent in troops to bring order to the region.

In general, the Tswana chiefs feared the Afrikaners, who were infamous for their mistreatment of Africans, more than they did the British. They welcomed British protection. Two Tswana chiefs, Sechele of the Kwena and Khama III of the Ngwato, had been converted to Christianity by British missionaries. They looked to the "tribe" those missionaries belonged to—that is, the British government—for protection from the chaos all around them. Because Sechele and Khama III controlled areas along the road north, their loyalty helped guarantee British control of that key area.

The Tswana chiefs were willing to accept nominal British rule over their region because it supported their authority, seemed to guarantee peace for their people, and offered protection from the Afrikaners. Because the British wanted control over the territory rather than power over the people, they were willing to use the existing Tswana social structures to implement their policies. For the moment the two sides had reached a workable compromise.

San Making Fire, c. 1910 *An indigenous people of southern Africa, the San are related to the Khoikhoi. They live mainly in Botswana, Nambia, and the northwestern part of Southwest Africa. San culture focused on the "band," which comprised several families (between 25 and 60 persons). Often all band members were related. Considerable interaction through trade and marriage occurred among the many bands although each band was an autonomous, somewhat leaderless unit within its own territory. In the late 20th century, some 42,000 San lived in Botswana. Namibia had about 35,000. A very small number were nomadic.*

TRIAL OF FAITH

Although some African groups, like the Griqua, generally tried to avoid conflict with Europeans, others chose to fight. For decades the Xhosa had seen their land in southeastern Africa shrink as Afrikaners claimed more and more of what had once been pasture for their herds. Although the Xhosa fought among themselves, they saw the Afrikaner threat as much more serious than any internal conflict. Cattle represented survival to the Xhosa. Without pasture, they could not raise their herds; and without their herds, they would starve.

EARLY CONFLICTS BETWEEN THE XHOSA AND THE WHITE SETTLERS

Faced with such a threat, the Xhosa went to war. In their first battles during the late 1700s, the Xhosa held their ground. Afrikaners were terrified as reports of destroyed farmsteads spread among the colonists. Meanwhile, the British had taken over the Cape Colony. Colonel Richard Collins decided to bring a temporary halt to the problems in the eastern frontier by separating the white and black populations. In 1811 and 1812 armed units attacked the Xhosa and drove them northeast across the Fish River. They burned crops and villages and made off with thousands of cattle.

The British wanted white settlers to stay southwest of the Fish River and the Xhosa to remain northeast of it.

The loss of so many cattle was a serious blow to the Xhosa, and their confinement in a much smaller area made life still more difficult. The British supported the chief of the Ngqika tribe and treated him as if he were supreme ruler of all the Xhosa. They held him personally responsible for keeping the Xhosa from crossing the Fish River and seizing settlers' cattle. This went against Xhosa tradition, which identified the chief of the Gcaleka as their supreme chief. As a result the Ngqika lost standing among the Xhosa people. In 1818 the Gcaleka and the Ndlambe joined forces in a successful attack on the Ngqika. Then they turned their attention to the settlers.

In 1819 between 9,000 and 10,000 Xhosa attacked Grahamstown. In part they were led by military commanders, but they also followed a diviner and prophet named Makanda. At first the Xhosa were successful. They almost overwhelmed the colonial forces. Then the whites gained the upper hand. When the Xhosa attack failed, Makanda gave himself up to the enemy. The British claimed the territory that lay between the Fish River and the Keiskamma River. They wanted it to be a "neutral belt" that would keep the settlers and Xhosa further from each other. The next year Makanda drowned while trying to escape from the prison on Robben Island. For decades the Xhosa waited in vain for his return.

During the 1820s the Xhosa faced even more crowded conditions. The British government gave up on its attempts to keep the settlers from crossing the Fish River. Missionaries and traders spread throughout Xhosa territory and some Xhosa began working a few months at a time for white farmers. At the same time thousands of Mfengu refugees poured into Xhosaland from Natal, where they had been forced out by the Zulus. Although the Xhosa welcomed the Mfengu, they looked down on them because the Mfengu didn't own any land. Understandably, the Mfengu didn't feel much loyalty toward the Xhosa.

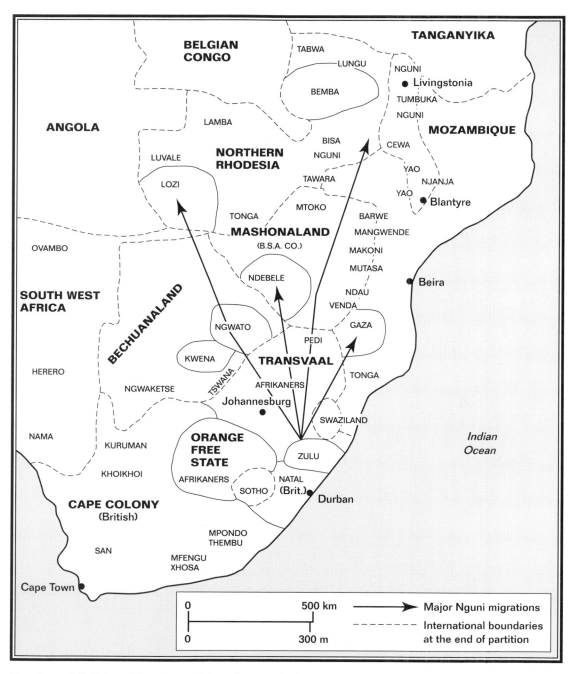

Peoples and Politics of Southern Africa, *showing the Nguni migrations and the area of the Chimurenga.*

By the middle of the 1830s, relations between the Xhosa and the whites had greatly deteriorated. British settlers and government officials humiliated the various Xhosa chiefs in front of their people. White traders forced Xhosa traders out of business. In December 1834 the Xhosa chiefs decided to put aside their differences and once again attack the whites. They planned a massive invasion of the colony. At first they were successful in driving most of the British farmers away from their farms. Then British troops arrived, captured the Gcaleka chief Hintsa, whom the Xhosa revered as their senior chief, and killed him when he tried to escape. Many Mfengu betrayed the Xhosa and began fighting alongside the British troops. In September 1835 the other Xhosa chiefs conceded defeat.

This defeat cost the Xhosa even more land. The British claimed the land between the Keiskamma and Kei Rivers. This claim was overturned because of a lobbying effort by missionaries and other concerned individuals in Britain, but that reversal in policy didn't last long. The settlers were determined to reclaim the land between the two rivers.

War broke out again in 1846. The Xhosa became allied with nearby Thembu chiefdoms. Together, the Africans drove the colonial forces back beyond the Keiskamma River. The colonial forces retaliated by destroying Xhosa homes, cattle, crops, and grain reserves. Xhosa women and children faced mass starvation, so in 1847 the Xhosa chiefs asked for peace terms.

Harry Smith, who was responsible for the killing of Chief Hintsa 12 years earlier, had just been made governor of the Cape Colony. His terms for peace included reclaiming the land between the Keiskamma and Kei Rivers and setting it up as a separate colony, British Kaffraria. According to one report, he humiliated all the Xhosa chiefs by forcing them to publicly kiss his feet.

Smith wasn't done dealing with the Xhosa. He allowed Mfengu and white military veterans to settle between the Fish and Keiskamma Rivers, immediately to the west of British Kaffraria.

Bloemfotein, c. 1925 *Bloemfotein was founded in 1846 and served as the capital of the Orange Free State (the Boer Republic) until it was captured by British forces (1900) during the South African War (1899–1902). Afterward, Bloemfotein was the site of the final negotiations (1909) that led to the establishment of the Union of South Africa (1910). Today, it is the judicial center of the Republic of South Africa.*

And he placed white magistrates over the Xhosa chiefs living in British Kaffraria. He summarily removed Sandile as the senior Ngqika chief and replaced him with the son of a British missionary. The Xhosa soon reached their limit in tolerating such outside interference with their way of life.

THE WITCH-FINDER MLANJENI

In 1850 a young man named Mlanjeni developed a reputation as a witch-finder. He called for young men throughout the Xhosa to cleanse themselves of witchcraft and sorcery. As his authority grew, he called for all the dun- and cream-colored cattle throughout Xhosa country to be sacrificed. In a nation of herders, where cattle was the foundation of the economy, such an act was a huge step of faith. But the Xhosa wanted the white people living in their section of southern Africa to leave. They obeyed Mlanjeni's instructions.

Mlanjeni was following traditional customs among the Xhosa. In preparing for battle young men first purified themselves from witchcraft. Then the Xhosa people made a sacrifice to the "shades," or powerful spirits. The third step was for the army to be treated by a war-doctor. Mlanjeni performed this ritual himself. He promised to make the warriors invulnerable to the white men's guns. If each warrior would sacrifice to the "shades" and wear the medicines Mlanjeni gave them, the bullets in the white men's guns would turn to water and the Xhosa would drive the whites out of their country.

About 20,000 Xhosa and various African allies went to war. As had happened during every Xhosa war in the 1800s, at first things went well. Once again, however, the colonial troops systematically destroyed Xhosa food supplies. At the end of the two-year war, the Xhosa were defeated.

The Xhosa were forced to relocate on smaller areas of land within British Kaffraria. George Grey became the new governor in December 1854. He developed a program similar to one he had used in dealing with the Maori in New Zealand. The various Xhosa chiefs were made salaried officials who reported to white magistrates. Missions, schools, hospitals, and employment on public works projects such as roads and irrigation ditches were organized to teach the Xhosa how to become "civilized." White settlements were located between Xhosa landholdings, so the Xhosa would have the example of "civilized" people to follow.

Almost immediately, a lethal cattle disease from Europe spread rapidly through the Xhosa herds. The Xhosa responded in two ways. They tried to control the movements of sick animals, and they held certain individuals responsible for the calamity. These people were executed as witches. Neither response helped. Every Xhosa chiefdom was affected by the loss of cattle. Some chiefdoms lost more than 80 percent of their herds.

The Xhosa were desperate. They had lost most of their land and cattle. As their world disintegrated and famine killed more and more of their people, they looked for a way to protect themselves from further calamities. At the same time they sought to preserve some part of their former way of life.

NONGQAUSE'S VISIONS

They turned to their traditional beliefs for answers. The Xhosa had heard rumors about the Crimean War that the British were fighting in Europe. They believed the Russians were black people who might come and help them defeat the English. Then a 16-year-old girl named Nongqause began having visions. Young, female visionaries had an honored place in Xhosa society and were often placed under the care of a senior diviner. In March 1856 she told her uncle Mhlakaza that she had seen strange people and cattle. Mhlakaza himself was a highly esteemed seer who held a role similar to that of Mlanjeni a few years earlier.

Mhlakaza also had visions. He saw a number of black people, among whom he recognized his dead brother. They said that they were the Russians who had been fighting the English and that they were now ready to wage war against the English in Africa. Before they could do anything, however, the Xhosa must destroy witchcraft and all of their cattle and grain as well as refrain from planting any seed.

To a point this vision was in keeping with Xhosa tradition. They believed that witchcraft was the cause of death and that once it was destroyed, people would be immortal. Destroying their sources of food, however, was a significant departure from tradition. Nongqause, her uncle, and other people who made prophecies in response to Nongqause's vision said that if the Xhosa obeyed, ancient heroes would rise from the dead and old people would have their youth restored. English cattle would replace those that had been sacrificed, and the Xhosa would receive more grain, wagons, clothes, guns, and ammunition than they needed. Most importantly, a great wind would drive the whites into the sea, and unbelievers would be destroyed as well.

These visions created a major rift within the Xhosa people. Families divided over whether to believe the prophecies or not. Those who believed were called *amathamba,* or "soft believers." Those who did not were called *amagogotya,* or "hard unbelievers." The unbelievers thought of themselves as sensible people, but those who believed saw the unbelievers as selfish cowards.

In October 1856 the leaders proclaimed that the Xhosa cattle must be killed within eight days. On the eighth day the dead would be resurrected. Thousands of cattle were slaughtered. The Xhosa people waited. Nothing happened. When the dead did not appear, the believers blamed the unbelievers. More cattle were killed. The date for the arrival of the ancestors kept changing. By February 1857 Xhosa throughout the countryside were starving. Mission stations and hospitals began to provide relief. The bishops of Cape Town and Grahamstown organized a relief society to distribute food and to nurse the sick.

It was not enough. By the end of January 1858, an estimated 400,000 head of cattle had been destroyed and at least 40,000

Xhosa had starved to death, although some estimates place the death toll much higher. Tens of thousands of Xhosa moved to the Cape Colony, where they took jobs on white farms or in towns and villages.

THE CONQUERED XHOSA

At the beginning of 1866, British Kaffraria became part of the Cape Colony. The Xhosa who remained didn't own enough land to survive. They had no choice but to become a labor force for the white farmers. Some Gcaleka Xhosa as well as their allies, the Thembu, managed to retain some independence in an area further north, known as the Transkei. For most Xhosa, however, decades of cattle disease, military defeats, and the cattle killing had transformed their beliefs and culture.

Tiyo Soga was a Xhosa commoner who was educated in Scotland. He married a Scottish woman and became a minister of the Scottish Presbyterian church. When he returned to southern Africa in the 1860s and saw what had happened to his people, he made it his mission to show them how to adapt to their position as a conquered people in a capitalist economy.

"The country of the Kafirs is now forfeited and the greater part of it has been given out in grants to European farmers," he wrote of his people's land. "I see plainly that unless the rising generation is trained to some of the useful arts, nothing else will raise our people, and they must be grooms, drivers of wagons, hewers of wood, or general servants. But let our youth be taught trades, to earn money, and they will increase and purchase land. When a people are not land-proprietors, they are of no consequence in this country and are tenants on mere sufferance." Future decades were to show how prophetic his words truly were.

Guide, Chobe River, c. 1910 *This guide accompanied Chauncy Stigand on his hunting expedition along the Chobe River, c. 1910. In 1885 the British proclaimed a protectorate over the Tswana and Kalahari peoples in what today is Botswana. In 1890 they extended the protectorate north to the Chobe River. Angola borders the area on the north and the Okavanga River is on the west. The main inhabitants of the Chobe River area are Bantu and San people. Dense forests and marshes make travel extremely difficult.*

6

A WARRING NATION

Europeans were not the only forces disrupting African life during the 19th century. Land that could be cultivated or used for grazing livestock was disappearing as chiefdoms multiplied in southeastern Africa. Africans increasingly found themselves hemmed in by mountain ranges, the Indian Ocean, the Kalahari Desert, and the Afrikaners.

DINGISWAYO, CHIEF OF THE MTHETHWA

In the late 1700s Dingiswayo became chief of the Mthethwa, one group within the Nguni people. They lived between the Indian Ocean and the Mfolozi and Mhlatuzi Rivers. Dingiswayo completely reorganized his chiefdom by combining the educational and military institutions. All the young men served in something like a standing army. It was organized in regiments made up of people roughly the same age. Each "age regiment" had a special uniform and used uniquely colored animal-hide shields.

With his powerful new military force, Dingiswayo slowly took control of most nearby chiefdoms. Generations of tribal quarreling came to an abrupt end. This new era of peace was used to justify his conquests.

Soon, just the threat of military action could persuade a chiefdom to surrender. When battles did take place, Dingiswayo was careful to protect women and children. He also allowed ruling families to stay in power, as long as one member pledged their loyalty to him. Life either improved or stayed much the same in the conquered chiefdoms, even though the young men now became part of Dingiswayo's army.

SHAKA AND THE POWERFUL ZULU NATION

The 2,000-member Zulu chiefdom was one of those absorbed by Dingiswayo. The Zulus lived between the upper Mhlatuzi River and the White Mfolozi River, west of the original Mthethwa territory. The Zulu chief Senzangakona had an illegitimate child named Shaka. After both mother and child were sent away by the chief, Shaka spent most of his youth among his mother's people. At 16 he went to work as a herdboy for some Mthethwa relatives. They placed him in Dingiswayo's army when he was about 22.

Shaka became an outstanding warrior with keen insights into military strategy. He rose through the ranks and became commander of his regiment. In 1816 chief Senzangakona died and power passed to one of his sons. Dingiswayo's inner circle had the new chief killed and replaced him with Shaka.

Shaka adapted the Mthethwa military system to the Zulus. He armed each Zulu warrior with a short stabbing spear specially designed for hand-to-hand combat. He taught his men how to surround and overwhelm the enemy, using merciless tactics that killed women and children along with warriors. Shaka was particularly careful to slaughter all the members of the ruling family. Survivors were incorporated into Zulu

Guides, Okavango River, c. 1910 *These guides accompanied Chauncy Stigand on his Okavango River hunting expedition, c. 1910. Many of the specimens from this trip are now on display in London's Natural History Museum. Notice how poles were used to propel the dugout canoes in the shallow marshy waters.*

society. Captured cattle and other wealth were distributed among the military regiments. Warriors shared in the wealth and could use the cattle's milk, but everyone knew that the cattle belonged to Shaka.

Shaka carefully avoided any moves against his old mentor Dingiswayo. When Dingiswayo was killed in 1818, however, Shaka killed Dingiswayo's heir and made one of his own loyal followers the new chief of the Mthethwa. The Mthethwa soon became part of the Zulu nation, as did most of the other independent chiefdoms in the area.

Shaka himself was the center of power in the Zulu nation. He was the sole source of laws and the only court of appeal. He made all the important military decisions and even acted as high priest for his people. Although he regularly sought advice from a small group of councilors who owed everything to him, Shaka made all the final decisions. He used traditional magic and feast-day celebrations to strengthen Zulu identity and pride. As each new chiefdom was absorbed into the Zulu nation, its language was replaced with the Zulu dialect. Every member of the nation owed his or her allegiance to Shaka, and those who appeared disloyal were easy targets for his executioners.

THE MFECANE

During Shaka's reign, one-fifth of the African continent felt the impact of Zulu nationalism. In the 1820s his army conducted annual campaigns to the north and south. This was the beginning of what the Zulus called the *Mfecane* and other African groups called the *Difaqane*.

As Shaka's power increased, he became more capricious, killing subjects on the slightest whim. When his mother died in 1827, Shaka encouraged a wave of mass hysteria that resulted in the deaths of hundreds of innocent people. Family members then plotted to overthrow Shaka. On September 24, 1828, he was assassinated by two half brothers, assisted by Shaka's personal servant.

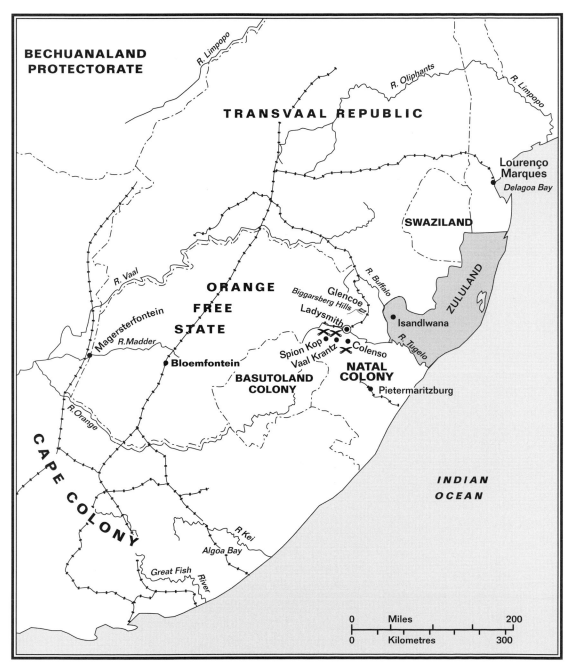

Zululand, 1899–1902.

Even after Shaka's reign ended, the *Mfecane* continued. By the early 1830s many chiefdoms in southern Africa had simply disappeared. Thousands were dead, and thousands more were homeless. In desperation, starving people turned to cannibalism simply to survive. Refugees from the annual attacks flooded the Cape Colony, where they could survive only by working for whites. Other refugees crowded into land already occupied by groups such as the Xhosa.

The *Mfecane* gave white settlers the false impression that Natal, the area south of the Zulus, was uninhabited. African survivors in the area hid from the new white arrivals, who were mostly Afrikaners from the British-controlled Cape Colony. What these white settlers didn't realize, however, was that the Zulu, Ndebele, Swazi, and Sotho kingdoms all claimed authority over this region.

DINGANE'S PREEMPTIVE STRIKE

The Zulus concluded that the white immigrants were a threat to Zulu safety, especially after the Afrikaners defeated the Ndebele and bragged about this conquest to the Zulus. So the Zulu king Dingane and his advisers decided to make a preemptive strike. On February 6, 1838, they invited Piet Rief and his party of Afrikaners to celebrate the signing of a treaty between the two groups. Once the unarmed party arrived, Dingane's warriors clubbed them to death. Zulu impis (regiments) then attacked the rest of the Afrikaner camps in the area. This action resulted in the deaths of an additional 40 white men, 56 white women, 185 white children, and more than 200 African or mixed-race servants.

The Zulus thought they were in charge, but on December 15, 1838, Andries Pretorius led a group of 57 wagons into the Zulu kingdom. They stopped at a defensively strategic position near the Ncome River, where they lashed their wagons together and prepared for battle. The next day 10,000 Zulus attacked. But their spears were no match for the Afrikaners' guns. The Zulus retreated after losing about 3,000 warriors. Not one Afrikaner was killed.

Mpande, the Peace Maker

This stunning defeat split the Zulu kingdom. Dingane's brother Mpande formed an alliance with the Afrikaners and defeated Dingane in battle. Dingane fled to the north, where he was killed by the Swazi. Pretorius proclaimed Mpande king of the Zulu, with the clear understanding that the Afrikaners in Natal now controlled the Zulu nation. The Zulus were confined to an area north of the Tugela River, and the Afrikaners occupied Natal. When the British took over control of Natal in 1843, the Zulus regained independence.

To ensure Zulu survival, Mpande took great pains to avoid offending any white people. The Zulu population grew, as did its cattle herds. Unlike his predecessors, Mpande did not force the members of conquered chiefdoms to remain part of the Zulu nation. Most were quite happy to do so, but those who objected were free to cross the Buffalo-Tugela River in search of their former homelands in Natal.

Cetshwayo, the Successor to Mpande

As Mpande created peace among the Zulus, war broke out in his own family. Both of his oldest sons, Cetshwayo and Mbuyazi, established small armies of young warriors as they maneuvered to succeed their father. The disruptions from this conflict intensified as Afrikaner farmers migrated into the area from the Transvaal to the north and British traders infiltrated from Natal to the south. In 1856 a huge battle took place next to the Tugela River. Cetshwayo defeated his brother. Thousands of people who had followed Mbuyazi fled across the river to Natal, adding to an already large black population in the colony. According to estimates, by 1870 the ratio of Africans to whites in Natal was 15 to 1.

Having won the right to succeed his father, Cetshwayo performed many of his father's duties. By the time Mpande died in 1872, Zulu society was once again stable and had regained great wealth in cattle. Cetshwayo was very popular. Although no opposition to his taking complete control of the Zulu nation had surfaced, relatives of Mbuyazi still lived in Zululand.

Realizing these people were potential rebels, Cetshwayo revitalized the army. Once again all young men were forced to join the army and live in regimental barracks. They became supremely confident of their abilities.

Very few whites lived in the Zulu kingdom. Most of them were missionaries, and they were not perceived as a threat. John Dunn, a Scot, had worked to develop a good relationship with the king. Cetshwayo made him a district chief in the south of the kingdom and used him as an intermediary with the Natal government. Dunn also made himself useful as a gunrunner.

Cetshwayo followed his father's policy of pursuing an alliance with British-controlled Natal to provide protection from the Afrikaners in the Transvaal. As part of that strategy, he invited Theophilus Shepstone to come to his coronation in 1873.

The Defeat of the Zulus

Changing politics, however, destroyed this long-standing policy. The British annexed the Transvaal, and Shepstone sided with the Afrikaners. Not long after this development, Chelmsford invaded Zululand with the intent of conquering it.

The Zulus were initially successful in turning back the British, but they used hand-to-hand fighting techniques that had not changed since the days of Shaka. Once the British learned to use their superior fire power, they seldom provided opportunities for one-on-one combat. When the Zulu warriors tried to get close enough to use their short spears, they became easy targets and suffered heavy losses.

John Dunn assessed the situation and, along with all his followers, sided with the British. Cetshwayo's cousin Hamu soon followed. The capital of Ulundi went up in flames on July 4, 1879. At that point the Zulu army ceased to exist. Cetshwayo was captured and sent to Cape Town. The British divided Zululand into 13 territories under 13 chiefs. Because the British resident who was to resolve all disputes had no legal or physical means for enforcing his decisions, the Zulus were soon at war with each other.

A Warring Nation

By 1882 the Zulus, British church leaders, and newspapers were calling for Cetshwayo's reinstatement. The deposed leader was allowed to visit Queen Victoria, and he was warmly received by the British public. When he returned to Africa, however, Cetshwayo was given control of only some of the Zulu people. During his absence he had lost authority. It did not take long for him to be defeated by other Zulus. He fled the area and died in 1884.

The British saw the defeat of the Zulus as a triumph of civilization over barbarism. Theophilus Shepstone had hoped that Cetshwayo's warriors would surrender their spears and become laborers working for wages. That process was about to begin.

Diamond Mine, 200 Feet Underground, c. 1910 *By 1889, diamond mining had become a monopoly controlled by Cecil Rhodes and the De Beers Consolidated Mines Company. While white men were employed as overseers or skilled workers, the workforce consisted of African migrant workers who lived in seventeen closed company compounds. On about four acres, each compound housed some 3,000 "workers." Fences ten feet high surrounded each compound and a fine wire netting stretched over the top. Large iron cabins, divided into rooms 25 feet x 30 feet, housed about thirty workers who slept on wooden bunk beds. Each room had a latrine. There was one large concrete bath in each compound. A white manager enforced order. Every worker signed a written contract with De Beers stating that he would "faithfully" work for at least three months—obviously pro forma as most were unable to read. Lung diseases, especially pneumonia, were common. No worker was permitted to leave the compound except to go to the mine under strict supervision. To prevent the swallowing of a rough diamond when a contract ended, workers were placed together naked in a room holding about 200 men. Their body wastes were watched for seven days as a final search.*

7

BROKEN PROMISES

The British were not satisfied with simply subduing the Zulu nation. They also wanted to subjugate ethnic groups living along the northern shore of the Zambezi River. The Zambezi, meaning "great river," is the fourth largest river of the African continent. It includes along its course Victoria Falls, one of the world's greatest natural wonders. The economy and survival of the Kololo/Lozi and the Ndebele, both Bantu-speaking ethnic groups, depended on this river. As the British government became more familiar with the resources available near the Zambezi, its desire to control African ethnic groups living near that river increased.

LIVINGSTONE AND SEBETWANE, THE KOLOLO/LOZI KING

British contact with the Kololo/Lozi began in 1851, when David Livingstone was exploring the Zambezi River. He met Sebetwane, the powerful African king of the Kololo/Lozi. Sebetwane had created a strong union of various tribes in what is now western Zambia, formerly known as Barotseland. Sebetwane recounted to Livingstone the history of the peoples he ruled—their wars, religion, customs, and traditions. He described the horrors of the *Mfecane* in the 1820s and 1830s, and how the

Bantu Hut, Transvaal, 1890 *H. F. Gros, a Boer photographer, compiled* Pictorial Description of the Transvaal *(1891). His photographs are a superb visual record of how people lived in the Transvaal before complete European domination. Gros gave his photographic collection to the Royal Geographical Society in 1893.*

Zulu warriors had forced his people, the Kololo, north through the treacherous Kalahari Desert to the Zambezi River.

Sebetwane then told Livingstone how he had defeated the Lozi, a group of more than 20 peoples who lived along the Zambezi. He gained their loyalty through a fair and just system of delegating authority to the conquered chiefs. Sebetwane also repelled two major attacks by the Ndebele, their militaristic neighbors, thereby further gaining the respect of the Lozi.

Sebetwane died the same year he met Livingstone, who was most impressed by this African warrior and statesman. The explorer's journals and detailed account of his encounter with Sebetwane remain an important source of information about the

Mfecane and its impact on southern Africa. By preserving the oral tradition, or spoken history, of Sebetwane's people, Livingstone gave historians material they use to understand African experiences from the perspective of Africans.

After Sebetwane's death in 1851, a succession of civil wars between rivals claiming his throne devastated western Zambia. The Kololo empire fell apart. Within a few years nothing remained to show the former prosperity of Sebetwane's realm. Where cattle had grazed and farmers had tilled the soil, wild beasts roamed. To use an African expression, "There were no lords but the lions."

THE UNITING OF THE LOZI AND OTHER TRIBES BY LEWANIKA

Finally in 1876 Lewanika united about 25 tribes, the Lozi being the dominant one. Lewanika followed Sebetwane's example by delegating power to the various peoples he ruled. This united the disparate tribes of his kingdom. He also reintroduced a shared heritage of traditional rituals such as the *Kuomboka,* meaning "to get out of the water." Every year as the waters of the Zambezi rose, the Lozi moved to higher ground. This migration was ritualized into an elaborate ceremony. The king and his followers paddled richly decorated barges from the submerged capital to the site of the winter palace. Performers greeted them with music—flutes, horns, bells, and the kalimma, a piano made of steel strips attached to a board and vibrated by the fingers.

This ceremony is still performed as a vivid reminder of Zambian cultural history. The Kuomboka ceremony was based on the dominant reality of Lozi life. They lived on a floodplain. Each year the people moved between two sets of villages, seeking higher ground during the months when the Zambezi overflowed its banks. They saw the varying water levels as an opportunity. They made skillful use of different soil and grass conditions to develop a complex agricultural economy. Theirs was a prosperous and generally peaceful land.

Throughout Lewanika's reign (1876–1916), the Lozi increasingly interacted with Europeans. British administrators thought the Lozi "aquatic display," as they termed the *Kuomboka,* a wonderful entertainment for visiting dignitaries. Lewanika even adapted the traditional ceremony in response to British wishes. He also welcomed missionaries, seeing them as advocates for his people.

THE LOZI PROTECTORATE

In 1890 Lewanika formally appealed for British protection. He knew how British troops defended King Khama III in Bechuanaland, an area to the south. Lewanika wanted similar protection from the Portuguese to the west and from the Ndebele to the east. The British expansionists were elated. They wired Cecil Rhodes to handle the details.

Rhodes saw a Lozi protectorate as another step toward fulfilling his goal of building a railway from the Cape to Cairo. The real needs of the Lozi were not his concern; his main interest was control of the north bank of the Zambezi River.

In 1890 Lewanika signed a protectorate treaty with Rhodes's British South Africa Company, which acted as the agent for the British government. Initially, all went well. Rhodes tried to keep the peace between the Lozi and their rival, the Ndebele. As long as peace could be maintained, the security costs of building his railroad toward Cairo would be minimal. If war broke out, then Rhodes would be forced to hire armed guards at an astronomical cost to protect his workers, who were preparing to lay down railway track nearing the difficult terrain of Central Africa.

THE CRUSHING OF THE NDEBELE

For his part the Ndebele chief Lobengula had no interest in fighting the superior British troops. He knew about the crushing defeat of more than 40,000 Zulu warriors by the British in 1879. Lobengula allowed his young warriors to make periodic raids so that they could hone their military

An Eastern Bantu Child, 1908 *Today, there are approximately 60 million speakers of the more than 200 distinct languages of the Bantu group. The eastern Bantu live in the Transvaal region of South Africa.*

skills, but he gave strict orders for his soldiers to avoid the white men's property.

When Ndebele warriors began periodically crossing into Lewanika's territory and attacking the Lozi people, Rhodes and the BSAC looked the other way in spite of the promises made to the Lozi in the protectorate treaty. To them maintaining Lozi safety was not worth the cost of fighting the Ndebele.

Then in June 1893 Ndebele warriors attacked the Shona, another Bantu-speaking people who lived on land owned by the British South Africa Company in eastern Zimbabwe. More than 400 Shona were killed in this dispute about cattle ownership. Because the attack had taken place on land owned by white people, the Ndebele warriors had gone against chief Lobengula's direct orders.

Leander Jameson, a friend and collaborator of Cecil Rhodes's, saw this attack as an opportunity. On Rhodes's behalf, Jameson had previously undertaken missions in 1889 and 1890 to charm the Ndebele chief Lobengula into making farming and mineral concessions to the British South Africa Company. In July 1893, after the raid against the Shona, which had occurred on company property and violated white men's property rights, Jameson urged Rhodes to use the event as an excuse to wipe out the Ndebele. Not only could the railroad then move northward, but the company could also seize the goldfields recently discovered within the Ndebele kingdom.

The Ndebele chief Lobengula admitted his error and even disavowed his own warriors. Nevertheless British troops ruthlessly crushed the Ndebele. By November 1893 the lands of Lobengula were incorporated under Jameson's authority to create the colony of Rhodesia.

Before he swallowed poison to avoid capture, Lobengula is said to have warned his people: "Your masters are coming. You will have to pull and shove their wagons. I did not want to fight with them." He was buried in a sitting position, wrapped in the skin of a black ox, the sign of a great leader.

Roan Antelope, Botswana, c. 1910 *Pictured here is Chauncy Stigand's guide standing beside a roan antelope. The roan is found in
small groups on South African plains and scrublands.*

BRITISH CONTROL OF THE ZAMBEZI RIVER'S NORTHERN SHORE

By the late 1890s Rhodes's British South Africa Company had gained control of the northern part of the Zambezi River. Lewanika and the Lozi had protected status, and the Ndebele had been permanently removed as a threat to the railroad. Over the next decade Lewanika was little by little forced to surrender Lozi natural resources and much of his remaining power.

Changing political power was disruptive for African groups during the 1890s. In addition three natural disasters also struck the Zambezi River area during that decade. In 1890, locusts appeared. These destructive grasshoppers travel in swarms, eating and totally destroying grain crops. Once begun, a locust plague is impossible to stop. Within five years, the number of locusts near the Zambezi had grown so large that they seemed like dark clouds spread across the sky, blotting out the sun. Then in 1894 a severe drought struck. Both humans and animals died in record numbers. Rinderpest, a highly contagious and fatal animal viral disease, was the third calamity. It attacked the lungs of cattle, sheep, goats, and other animals. By 1898 most cattle along the Zambezi were dead.

Without crops or cattle, the Lozi, the surviving Ndebele, and thousands of other Africans in the region were forced to take wage-paying jobs from white people. These Africans built railways and roads. They left their tribal lands to work the great gold and diamond mines. Hunting, herding, and other traditional ways of life all but disappeared. Many Africans sensed that the white presence, like the natural calamities, would be disastrous to their way of life.

Lozi also became migrant workers. They traveled south on Cecil Rhodes's railroad, seeking jobs. Such migratory laborers no longer had daily contact with their elders, further undermining the authority of Lewanika and local leaders. Young Lozi became exposed to European education, and some became British civil servants working throughout southern Africa.

Lewanika's hope to control the spread of modernization within his nation never materialized. The ways of the Lozi ancestors continued to be undermined. In 1906 the British insisted that serfdom and slavery among the Lozi stop. This action brought an end to the traditional methods for cultivating the floodplain on which Lozi agriculture depended, so farming in the floodplain virtually ceased.

Lewanika's lands gradually became politically and economically absorbed by South Africa. Lewanika died in 1916, a virtual prisoner of the British in his own home.

Tswana Creamery, Southern Botswana, c. 1920 *Traditional Tswana foods include dried caterpillars, wild plums, and beer made from millet.*

A DISUNITED WHOLE

As the 1890s ended, Great Britain became obsessed with dominating the Afrikaners in southern Africa. Much of that determination was focused on the Transvaal, or South African Republic, as it was then called. As had happened through much of the last quarter of the century, Cecil Rhodes was deeply involved in plans to bring the South African Republic under British rule. Rhodes was prime minister of the Cape Colony. More than ever, he did not trust the British government to take action. So in 1895 he hatched a plot to stage a coup in the Transvaal, which would force the British government to intervene and support the revolution.

THE JAMESON RAID

Who would want to start a coup in the South African Republic? The region had been settled by Afrikaners and they largely controlled the government; gold and diamond mining, however, had caused a huge influx of whites from European nations, the United States, and other parts of Southern Africa. Afrikaners were mostly farmers who followed a strict form of Calvinist Christianity. Recent immigrants, known as *Uitlanders* (literally, "outsiders"), rarely became citizens but they outnumbered the Afrikaners. The Uitlanders had varied ethnic backgrounds, religious beliefs, and

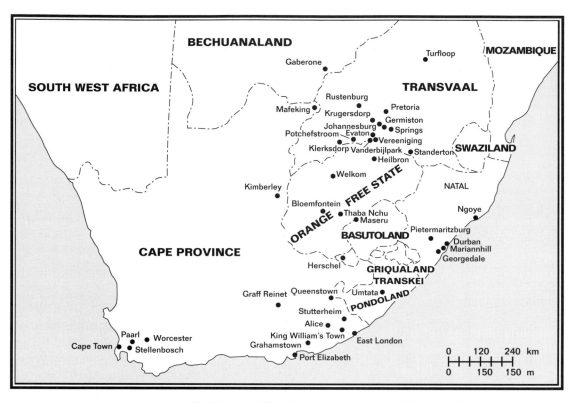

Politics and Nationalism in South Africa, 1919–35 *(after G. M. Gerhard, 1978)*

economic resources. They complained about the high cost of living, bureaucratic corruption, and outrageous prices for mining supplies, resulting from government-granted monopolies on everything from dynamite to railroad transport. Their protests were becoming louder and longer.

Leander Jameson, who had masterminded the attack on the Ndebele earlier in the decade, organized the coup in the South African Republic. He secretly worked with the Uitlanders in Johannesburg. This small group organized other Uitlanders to seize control of Johannesburg. Jameson would then enter the South African Republic with British South Africa Company police from Bechuanaland. Ultimately, the region would become a British colony.

Iron Foundry, Mpumalanga, 1890 *The Mpumalanga region in eastern Transvaal contains one of the world's richest deposits of iron ore. The native population belongs mainly to the Nguni, a cluster of related Bantu-speaking ethnic groups living in South Africa. The Nguni dialect is unusual among Bantu languages in that it has "clicking" speech sounds. Today, the Nguni make up about 90 percent of the province's population. Whites make up 10 percent of the population. Four-fifths of them speak Afrikaans, the remainder English.*

Things went badly from the beginning. Conspirators fought among themselves over petty issues such as which flag to use. They weren't sure they could trust Rhodes and were unable to attract a large following. When Rhodes learned of this, he tried to warn Jameson to stay in Bechuanaland. Jameson, ignoring Rhodes, led 500 British South Africa Company police into the Transvaal. The disunited conspirators tried to take over Johannesburg while at the same time negotiating with Paul Kruger, president of the South African Republic. On January 2, 1896, Jameson and his policemen surrendered to Transvaal Afrikaners. Kruger commuted the Uitlanders' death sentences and handed over Jameson and his company police to British authorities.

The consequences of the Jameson Raid, as it came to be known, were enormous. Kruger tightened restrictions on political activities and purchased large quantities of arms in Europe. He strengthened his ties with the Afrikaner Orange Free State and won a huge majority in the 1898 South African Republic presidential election.

Jameson and five officers were convicted in British trials and received sentences of hard labor. Rhodes accepted responsibility for the plot and resigned as prime minister, but he retained his seat in the Cape parliament. Colonial Secretary Joseph Chamberlain threatened to revoke the charter for the British South Africa Company because of Rhodes's involvement in the plot. Rhodes wouldn't tolerate the loss of his company and, in turn, threatened Chamberlain. If Chamberlain revoked the charter, Rhodes vowed to make public the fact that Chamberlain had known about the raid before it took place. Such a revelation would ruin the colonial secretary's political career. The counterthreat worked; Chamberlain backed down. The charter for Rhodes's company was saved—as was Chamberlain's political future.

SETTING THE STAGE FOR THE SOUTH AFRICAN WAR

Although the British government tried to look like an innocent bystander, the Jameson Raid transformed politics in the

Cape Colony. For years Afrikaners and British had worked together in Cape politics. Now that relationship was severed. With few exceptions members of the Afrikaner Bond, who had represented a large part of Cecil Rhodes's base of support, rejected his leadership. They felt no British person could be trusted. The 1898 Cape Colony election brought a narrow victory to the Afrikaner Bond. William P. Schreiner formed the new government. Schreiner sought a peaceful settlement between the British and the Afrikaners. He failed.

Because the Jameson Raid had been a disaster, Joseph Chamberlain concluded that the only way for the British to control southern Africa was to somehow obtain cooperation with the Afrikaners. Unfortunately, the colonial secretary made three errors:

1. He believed that Afrikaner extremists were conspiring to take over the entire region.
2. He underestimated the willingness of the Afrikaners in the South African Republic to defend their country.
3. He appointed Alfred Milner, an inflexible British administrator and a fervent imperialist who wouldn't hesitate to lead the British to war, as high commissioner.

In reality the Afrikaners were perfectly satisfied to keep things as they were as long as the British did not threaten their control of the South African Republic. But after Paul Kruger's reelection in 1898, Milner began lobbying both in Britain and in southern Africa. He became fixated on creating a conflict that would require British military action. He obtained a petition with more than 21,000 signatures from the Uitlanders, calling for British intervention. He also dismissed a proposal by Schreiner, of the Cape Colony, to peacefully work out all disagreements. "What is at stake," Chamberlain proclaimed in a cabinet memorandum, "is the position of Britain in South Africa—and with it the estimate formed of our power and influence in our colonies and throughout the world." Military reinforcements were subsequently shipped to Africa.

At this point the leaders of the Afrikaners were convinced that Britain was determined to destroy their independence and would be satisfied with nothing less than the end of the South African Republic. The stage was set for the South African War. The Afrikaners called it the Second War of Freedom, because they had earlier fought for control of the Transvaal. The British called it the Boer War because they had long used the Dutch term *Boer* ("farmer") as a derogatory slur against the Afrikaners.

THE SOUTH AFRICAN WAR

When the war began in October 1899, the British thought it would end quickly. The Afrikaners would be unable to replenish their munitions because the British Royal Navy controlled the seas, and the Portuguese agreed to prevent arms from passing through Mozambique. Although the public in Europe and the United States largely sided with the Afrikaners, no foreign government could risk sending military aid to any group fighting Britain. The British were confident that they would ultimately overwhelm the Afrikaners. The Afrikaner republics had 88,000 fighting men, including overseas volunteers and colonists from the Cape. The British troops, in contrast, stood at just 20,000 when war broke out, but Britain mobilized 450,000 additional uniformed men before the conflict ended.

In spite of these British advantages, Great Britain was denied victory for more than two years. The Afrikaner republics held the initial advantage, but in 1900 the tide turned. The British occupied Bloemfontein, Johannesburg, and Pretoria—the three leading Afrikaner cities. President Kruger fled to Switzerland, where he died four years later. In December 1900 the British took control of the two Afrikaner republics and renamed them Transvaal and Orange River Colony.

The war seemed all but won. But once again the British had misjudged their enemy. The Afrikaners resorted to guerilla tactics. Organized in small units, they seized British supplies, overran small military units, and cut railroad tracks. In response, British Lord Kitchener adopted a scorched earth policy. He ordered that farmhouses of combatant Afrikaners be burned, livestock confiscated, crops destroyed, and their families herded into camps. Conditions in the camps were appalling, lacking the minimal requirements of enough food and clean water. Typhoid, dysentery, and measles were rampant. Most of the 28,000 Afrikaners who died in the camps were children. David Lloyd-George, leader of the British opposition party, compared Kitchener's tactics to those of Herod, who had also "attempted to crush a little race by killing its young sons and daughters." This suffering by the Afrikaners etched in their minds the belief that it was their God-given duty to survive as a people, regardless of the tribulations forced upon them.

Although the South African War was being waged between two groups of whites, Africans could not remain mere spectators during the three years of devastation and economic disruption. At first the British and the Afrikaners tacitly agreed not to involve Africans in the fighting except as servants and scouts. Gradually, however, blacks were used by both sides in the fighting. Almost 116,000 Africans were placed in Kitchener's camps. Of those, 14,000 died.

Peace of Vereeniging

On May 31, 1902, the Peace of Vereeniging was signed in Pretoria. Milner, because he was high commissioner, had a great deal of control over writing the treaty. He was determined to eradicate Afrikaner identity by ruling Afrikaners autocratically and flooding their lands with British settlers. Not until the British greatly outnumbered the Afrikaners did he plan on introducing any representative government. The Peace of Vereeniging included a major concession to both Afrikaner and British colonists: "The question of granting the franchise to natives will not be decided until after the introduction of self-government." In other words, the decision on whether to extend political rights to blacks would not be made until self-government was restored to the former Afrikaner republics. That one condition inevitably led to the disenfranchisement of all Africans in South Africa because most Afrikaners were not interested in allowing Africans to vote.

The war among the whites had brought only disillusion to the blacks. Racially discriminatory legislation previously passed by the Afrikaners was expanded by the British. State control of blacks intensified. Milner tightened the pass laws, which restricted the ability of Africans to move freely.

Mining companies continually cut wages for African workers and agreed among themselves what they would pay the Africans so there would be no competition for employees based on better salaries. When Africans walked off their jobs, the government used physical force to get them back to work. The government also brought in Chinese workers to undermine the Africans' negotiating position.

Milner's plans for eliminating the Afrikaner identity did not succeed. The difficulties Afrikaners had experienced during the war, the forced incarceration they had endured, and the deaths of so many of their children united the Afrikaners as never before. Although divisions still existed among the Afrikaners—as represented by their leaders Louis Botha and Jan Smuts—they put those differences aside in the larger interest of denouncing Milner. Political events in Britain, including controversy over the South African War, forced Milner out of power in 1905.

By 1907, 63,000 Chinese had come to southern Africa, further complicating the already tense racial situation. They worked as unskilled laborers in the mines for very low wages. That same year the British allowed an election in the Transvaal. Much to their surprise, Transvaal Afrikaners won control of the government. Similar results occurred nine months later in the Orange River Colony. Then in February 1908 John X.

Native Chiefs, Pretoria, 1881 *This is a remarkable photograph of "Soutpansberg Kafir Chiefs" and their interpreter. (In South Africa, "kafir" is used in a pejorative sense to mean any African black.) The photograph lists each chief's name and is dated "Pretoria, Augt. 1881."*

Merriman came to power in the Cape Colony with the support of the Afrikaner Bond. Of the four British colonies in southern Africa, only Natal remained sympathetic to British imperialism. And Natal, where Africans outnumbered whites by 10 to 1, felt the need of support from the other colonies to maintain white rule.

A Constitution for a United South Africa

As a result, in May 1908 the four colonies appointed delegates to a national convention with the purpose of creating a constitution for a united South Africa. Thirty white, male delegates—twelve from the Cape Colony, eight from the Transvaal, and five each from the Orange River Colony and Natal—submitted a constitution to the colonial parliaments within a year. All four colonies approved the document.

This constitution had profound effects on South African history for most of the 20th century. First, the constitution followed the British parliamentary model of government. Second, the constitution resolved differences in voting laws among the four colonies by restricting membership in the new parliament to white men, while allowing voting methods in each colony to stand. Third, the constitution stated that at regular intervals judicial commissions would divide the entire country into electoral divisions. These divisions would be used as voting districts to elect the lower house of parliament. Each division was to have roughly the same number of voters. (The precedent was the reapportionment clauses of the U.S. Constitution.) Fourth, the constitution made both Dutch and English the official languages of South Africa.

The constitution provided for the inclusion of Southern Rhodesia, Basutoland, Bechuanaland Protectorate, and Swaziland into the new nation at some future time. The draft constitution was sent to the British parliament for approval. A few parliament members objected to the exclusion of blacks, but the 1909 Union of South Africa Act passed, giving the new federation dominion status. On May 31, 1910, Afrikaner

A Disunited Whole

Louis Botha became prime minister of the Union of South Africa. This British dominion was made up of 4 million Africans; 500,000 coloreds (a term used to describe people of mixed white and African ancestry in southern Africa); 200,000 Indians and Chinese; and 1,275,000 whites, the majority being of Dutch ancestry. Many of those residents were not happy with the changes that had just taken place, and they were about to begin the long process of letting the world know about their grievances against the new Union of South Africa.

Interior of a Sotho Hut, c. 1910 *The Sotho are a linguistically and culturally distinct people who live in the grasslands of southern Africa. They rely both on cultivation and on animal husbandry. The typical settlement pattern was characterized by hamlets of large huts with mud-brick or stone walls surmounted by a thatched roof. Shown here is an example of wattle construction in which poles are interwoven with slender branches or reeds to form the building. Towns of considerable size occur among some groups of Sotho, particularly the Tswana.*

9

BEGINNINGS OF PROTEST

GANDHI'S NONVIOLENT PROTEST IN NATAL

Among those who were discontented with the new Union of South Africa was an Indian lawyer named Mohandas K. Gandhi. Born in India in 1869, Gandhi studied in London. He returned to India in 1891 to practice law, with little success. In 1893, at the age of 24, Gandhi went to Natal to do legal work for an Indian company for one year. Almost immediately, he was abused because he was an Indian who claimed rights as a British subject. During a journey to Pretoria, Gandhi was beaten by a white stagecoach driver because he refused to travel on the footboard to make room for a European passenger. Gandhi was also turned away from hotels marked "for Europeans only." He quickly observed that Indians throughout southern Africa suffered discrimination in every aspect of ordinary life.

Most Indians accepted this treatment, but Gandhi was repulsed by it. He resolved never again to accept an injustice. He was committed to defending his dignity both as an Indian and as a man. During his first year in southern Africa, he tried to explain to fellow Indians their rights and responsibilities, but he had no intention of staying in Natal once his contract expired.

In Durban in 1894, days before he was scheduled to return to India, Gandhi learned that the Natal Legislative Assembly was considering a bill that would deny

Indians the right to vote. Incensed, Gandhi canceled his travel plans. He launched a political campaign that included petitions to the Natal legislature and the British government. His actions failed to block passage of the bill, but Gandhi succeeded in drawing attention to how Natal treated its Indian population.

That same year, Gandhi founded the Natal Indian Congress, a political organization through which he organized the Indian community and publicized their cause to the world. In spite of the treatment of Indians in Natal, when the South African War broke out in 1899, Gandhi urged his fellow Indians to fight for the British. They were citizens of a British colony, claiming the rights of citizens. He also felt justice was on the British side. Gandhi did paramedic work. He was decorated by the British government for establishing a volunteer ambulance corps.

Most Natal Indians did assist the British, but the treatment Indians received across southern Africa did not change after the war. In 1906 the Transvaal government required Indians to register with the police, a requirement not made of European residents. That September Indians held a mass protest rally. With Gandhi as their leader, they pledged to peacefully defy the ordinance. This event is considered the birth of the nonviolent protest movement in the modern Western world.

Gandhi led many campaigns for Indian rights, including civil disobedience among Indian miners who protested the horrendous working conditions in the gold and diamond mines. He was arrested many times. Gradually, Gandhi developed a philosophy centered around the concept of nonviolence—and how, through courage, the discriminated could overcome fear to obtain their natural rights. He titled his autobiography *My Experiments with Truth.*

While the Indians were struggling for equal treatment, Africans were facing their own struggles. Many Africans were bitterly disappointed by the outcome of the South African War. They had fought for the British because British politicians had

Herero Woman, 1909 *Toward the end of the 19th century, the last areas of southern Africa not yet under European control fell to the colonialists. A relative newcomer to the colonial scene, Germany, claimed South West Africa in 1884 and proceeded to rule it with an iron hand. The first German administration succeeded in making treaties with the Herero and other local groups. Almost immediately, though, the Germans, who were now arriving as settlers, attempted to curb the authority of local chiefs. The newly arrived German farmers arrogantly occupied large tracts of land without the permission of Herero chiefs. European goods were sold on credit and Herero defaulters were often sentenced by a German court to work for their creditors. When an epidemic broke out among the cattle in 1896, the Germans, in an attempt to contain it, killed many Herero cattle and oxen. To the Herero, the oxen were important in ancestor worship. The Herero rebelled violently in 1904. The three-year war that followed cost more than 2,000 German lives and brought the Herero close to extinction. The German military leader, who signed his correspondence "the great general of the mighty Kaiser," ordered the Herero people exterminated. "Every Herero, whether found armed or unarmed, with or without cattle, will be shot. I shall not accept any more women or children," he vowed. Within the next few months, his orders were carried out with chilling efficiency. A German officer later commented that "the solemn silence of the territory echoed with the death-rattle of the dying, the shrieks of the maddened people." Only 16,000 out of an estimated 60,000 to 80,000 Herero survived the German onslaught.*

promised "equal laws, equal liberty" for all races once the Afrikaners were defeated. But the Treaty of Vereeniging brushed aside such promises. Mission-educated Africans, in particular, felt betrayed.

THE FOUNDING OF AFRICAN POLITICAL ORGANIZATIONS

The creation of several political organizations took place shortly after the Treaty of Vereeniging was signed. In 1902 the African Political Organization (APO) was founded. Later called the African People's Organization, it worked to unite Africans across ethnic and regional lines to fight against the formation of a white-ruled Union of South Africa. Colored people (a term used to describe people of mixed white and African ancestry in southern Africa) formed a separate Coloured Affairs Department.

Another political organization formed in 1902 was the South African Native Congress. Initially, it intended to coordinate African activities in the Cape Colony, especially those involving electoral politics. Other organizations existed in Natal, the Transvaal, and the Orange River Colony.

Action was not limited to the educated. In 1906 African peasants in Natal, led by chief Bambatha, refused to pay a poll tax, which was disproportionate to their earnings. This resistance developed into an armed uprising. When it was over (and the poll tax still stood) between 3,000 and 4,000 Africans had been killed and 7,000 had been thrown in jail.

As Africans observed white politicians moving toward unifying the four colonies, they decided to take their own action. In 1908, while the white colonists were holding their constitutional convention, African organizations throughout the four colonies as well as Bechuanaland held congresses at which they elected 60 delegates to attend the South African Native Convention in Bloemfontein. That convention was held from March 24 to March 26, 1909.

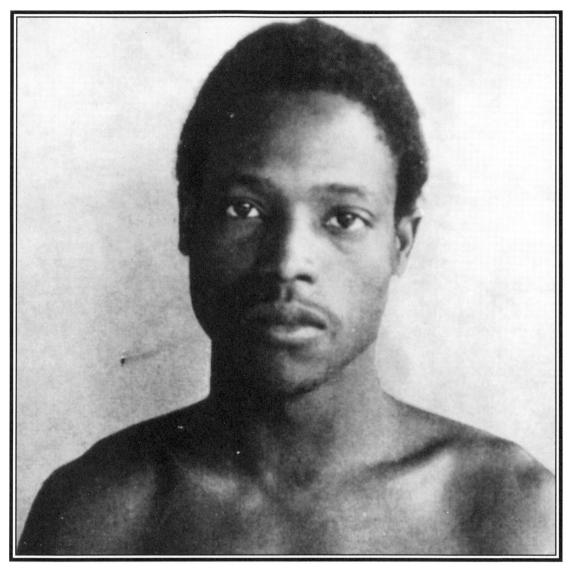

Herero Man, 1909 *This photograph was taken by Kurd Schwabe, a major sent to German South West Africa. Schwabe's three-volume study of the German protectorate graphically details the slaughter of the Herero during the 1904–1907 war. For almost a year, the Kaiser's armies crisscrossed the country- side in a relentless hunt for victims. Of the 16,000 Herero who survived, some 14,000 were placed in concentration camps to die. The Nama people, fairly prosperous sheep and cattle herders who lived in southern Namibia, also felt the wrath of German rule. Schwabe estimated that half of the Nama popu- lation, between 15,000 to 20,000, were wiped out between 1904 and 1907.*

During the convention, which was chaired by Walter Rubusana of the Cape delegation, people discussed the issues in the proposed constitution that directly related to African and colored people. These issues included neglecting to ensure voting rights for blacks in areas where voting rights did not yet exist and excluding nonwhites from becoming members of parliament. The convention passed resolutions in opposition to these elements of the constitution and authorized a deputation to travel to England and present their concerns. Members of the group included Rubusana, Gandhi, and Dr. Abdurahman, the leader of the African People's Organization.

The deputation was unable to change the British government's decision about the creation of the Union of South Africa. The South African Act of Union was passed by the British House of Commons in 1909 and ratified by the South African Parliament on May 31, 1910 (the eighth anniversary of the signing of the Treaty of Vereeniging).

THE AFRICAN NATIONAL CONGRESS

Realizing that they now had no voice in their government, educated Africans decided it was time to put aside their ethnic and historical differences so that they could act with a united front. In October 1911 Pixley ka Isaka Seme, one of the African leaders, wrote: "The demon of racialism, the aberrations of the Xhosa-Fingo feud, the animosity that exists between the Zulus and the Tongaas, between the Basutos and every other Native must be buried and forgotten; it has shed among us sufficient blood. We are one people. These divisions, these jealousies, are the cause of all our woes and of all our backwardness and ignorance today."

On January 8, 1912, representatives from the four provinces as well as from Botswana once again gathered in Bloemfontein. At their meeting they established the South

Tswana Chief, Palapye, c. 1929 *Between 1885 and 1890, the British proclaimed a protectorate over their Tswana allies. British colonial expansionists had to use the road—and later the railroad—through the protectorate to colonize Zimbabwe. The British divided the protectorate into eight largely self-administering tribal reserves and five white farm blocks, with the remainder classified as Crown, or state, lands. In the 1920s and 1930s, leading Tswana chiefs opposed British attempts to initiate mining development, claiming that it would only enhance colonial settlements. In 1977, South Africa created an "independent" Bantu homeland for the Tswana called Bophuthatswana, but it was never recognized by the international community.*

African Native National Congress, which was later to be called the African National Congress. This was the first permanent national organization dedicated to representing Africans and colored people in South Africa. Seme described their goals in his keynote address:

> Chiefs of royal blood and gentlemen of our race, we have gathered here to consider and discuss a theme which my colleagues and I have decided to place before you. We have discovered that in the land of their birth, Africans are treated as hewers of wood and drawers of water. The white people of this country have formed what is known as the Union of South Africa—a union in which we have no voice in the making of the laws and no part in their administration. We have called you therefore to this Conference so that we can together devise ways and means of forming our national union for the purpose of creating national unity and defending our rights and privileges.

The delegates appointed a committee to draw up a constitution. The committee included religious ministers, lawyers, an editor, a building contractor, teachers, an estate agent, and an interpreter and Native Labour Agent. They had been educated at mission schools, and five of them had studied abroad. While these committee members were relatively young (in their thirties to early fifties), the conference also respected tradition by appointing the seven paramount chiefs as honorary presidents. Included among these was Dinizulu, a Zulu chief who had been deposed and exiled by the British.

NATIVES LAND ACT

The need for such an organization was quickly apparent. In 1913 Louis Botha's South African party administration, without consulting any Africans, passed the Natives Land Act. It

San Men, c. 1920 *The indigenous San people once lived by hunting and food gathering. Most of the surviving San have been restricted to unattractive semiarid areas of South Africa because of encroaching European settlements and pressure from tribal Africans of other heritages. Today, most surviving San work for wages on European farms or continue in a long-standing relationship with other Africans whom they serve as hunters and cattle herders in return for food and clothing.*

prohibited Africans from purchasing or leasing any land outside the reserves from people who were not Africans. The reserves were lands dedicated to the Africans, and according to the act they totaled about 22 million acres—roughly 7 percent of the total area of South Africa. The Land Act also prohibited share-cropping in the Orange Free State. Because of increased population on the reserves, people living in the reserves after 1910 were unable to produce enough food to feed themselves. One of the results of the Natives Land Act of 1913 was that the reserves became pools of cheap, unskilled labor for white farmers and miners.

The land on the reserves became overgrazed and over-planted. Streams and waterholes dried up. Original vegetation disappeared. Soil erosion spread. Infrastructure such as roads and railways tended to bypass the reserves.

GANDHI'S LEGACY IN SOUTH AFRICA

While Africans were adjusting to these hardships, the small Indian minority also continued to face difficulties. That same year hundreds of Indians, including women, went to jail rather than comply with laws they believed to be unjust. Thousands of Indian workers in the mines went on strike, facing imprisonment, flogging, and execution, rather than continue to work under inhuman conditions. Gandhi continued to publicize their situation to the rest of the world. Under pressure from the governments of both Britain and India, the South African government accepted a compromise negotiated between Gandhi and South African Jan Christian Smuts.

In 1914 Gandhi left South Africa for India, where he continued his nonviolent protests. Both Africans and Indians had learned from Gandhi during his one-year stay that had ended up stretching across 21 years. Even his enemies respected him.

"The saint has left our shores," Smuts told a friend that summer, "I hope forever." Decades later he wrote that it had been his "fate to be the antagonist of a man for whom even then I had the highest respect."

Gandhi's work did not permanently solve the problems of Indians living in South Africa any more than did the founding of the South African Native National Congress solve the problems of Africans. The work that grew from these beginnings, however, was to transform the face of South Africa.

Tigerfish, Okavango Swamp, c. 1910 *The tigerfish is considered one of the finest freshwater sport fishes in the world because of its fierce combativeness when caught. It is ferocious, having sharp teeth that resemble those of a small shark.*

10

SOUTH AFRICA TRANSFORMED

T he 1910s and 1920s in South Africa were a time of great turmoil. Workers of all races went on a series of strikes that were put down by force. Antagonism between Afrikaners and British South Africans was further intensified by the Afrikaner Rebellion of 1914.

When Britain declared war on Germany in 1914, South Africa was automatically at war because of its dominion status. South African troops mobilized to invade German Southwest Africa. Retired Afrikaner generals protested this action. More than 11,000 men, mainly poor, rural Afrikaners, joined the uprising. The government sent 32,000 troops to end the Afrikaner Rebellion. More than 300 Afrikaners were killed.

THE RISE OF POLITICAL PARTIES

The resulting Afrikaner anger and resentment toward British South Africans built support for the National Party, founded by James Hertzog in 1914. In the next year's general election, the National Party won 30 percent of the vote. Afrikaners had begun to desert the South African Party led by Louis Botha and Jan Christian Smuts.

Hertzog and the National Party worked to increase their popularity. In 1920 the party won a majority of the votes, and in 1923 Hertzog's National Party formed a pact with the Labour Party and took power. This coalition government, known as the Pact government, advanced Afrikaner issues.

THE INCREASING SEGREGATION OF SOUTH AFRICAN LIFE

Although the National and South African Parties had their differences, they agreed on the necessity to maintain white power. Legislation passed in the 1910s and 1920s made segregation of all types a distinctive feature of South African life. Under the 1911 Mines and Works Act, certain jobs in mining and the railways were reserved for white workers. The Natives Land Act of 1913 restricted where black people could live. The Native Urban Areas Act of 1923 segregated urban residential space.

In response to these laws, the Industrial and Commercial Workers Union (ICU) called for land and liberation for Africans. Initially it experienced huge growth, but unable to improve conditions in the countryside, the ICU fell apart into feuding factions by 1929.

The growth of the ICU, however, sparked radicalism in other organizations, including the African National Congress (ANC). The Communist Party of South Africa, founded in 1921, began recruiting African members beginning in 1925.

Whites noticed these actions on the part of Africans, so for the first time questions of native policy dominated white politics in the 1929 general election. Afrikaner nationalists made "black peril" and "communist menace" rallying cries.

The election brought another victory to the National Party, which drew its main support from Afrikaner farmers and intellectuals. The major opposition party was the South African Party—the party of most English-speaking whites.

A worldwide depression caused serious problems in South Africa and eroded Hertzog's political strength. As a result he formed a coalition with Smuts and the South African Party in 1933. The two parties merged into the United Party. Hertzog and Smuts agreed on the necessity of continuing to advance whites at the expense of blacks.

Daniel F. Malan, a former Dutch Reformed minister, refused to participate in the merger of the two political parties. He formed a new Purified National Party. It became the opposition party in parliament.

In 1936 an overwhelming majority of the parliament voted to remove what few Africans still remained on the voting rolls. In exchange it allowed blacks in the Cape Province to elect three white representatives to the House of Assembly. Africans throughout the country indirectly elected four white senators. Parliament also created a Natives Representative Council.

As South Africa began to pull out of the depression, white farmers prospered and new businesses developed. Although conditions improved for whites, the same could not be said for other South Africans. In gold mining real wages of Africans declined by 15 percent between 1911 and 1941. White miners were paid 12 times as much as Africans.

The only education available to Africans was at Christian missions, which did not have the resources to provide schooling for all African children. A small but growing number of Africans earned degrees and became teachers, lower-level civil servants, or clergy. The ANC, APO, and South African Indian Congress, led by missionary-educated men, had little political influence.

The United Party split when Britain declared war on Germany on September 3, 1939. Hertzog wanted the country to remain neutral, but Smuts wanted South Africa to join with Britain. In a narrow vote Smuts and his allies won the debate, and Smuts became prime minister.

About 135,000 white South Africans fought in World War II, and 75,000 Africans and coloreds became laborers and transport drivers. Many Afrikaners, however, supported the racial views of Hitler, and some of them committed acts of sabotage. Malan and the Purified National Party gradually gained the support of Afrikaner clergy and intellectuals.

Because of its platinum, uranium, and steel resources, South Africa flourished economically during the war. Africans migrated to cities in greater numbers, and by the end of the war,

Tswana Hut Building, Southern Botswana, c. 1920 *Cylindrical mud bricks were used as the foundation for a traditional hut. Each brick is about 12 to 14 inches high and 10 inches wide. The circular dwelling had a conical thatched roof. Three or four huts made up a Tswana compound. Each was set around an open fireplace and surrounded by low clay walls.*

more Africans lived in cities than did whites. Because of restrictions on where they could live, these Africans built huge squatter camps. In 1946, 74,000 African gold miners went on strike, seeking better wages and living conditions. The white government brutally suppressed the strike.

POSTWAR SEGREGATION LAWS CREATE THE APARTHEID SYSTEM

Members of the United Party expected to win the 1948 election easily; instead they were narrowly defeated by Malan's National Party. Hendrik F. Verwoerd was among those elected to the senate that year. He believed the South African population was made up of four distinct racial groups: white, African, colored, and Asian. He thought whites had the right to control the state because they were the only "civilized" group. More than any other person, he was responsible for putting these views into the laws that created the apartheid system.

The Population Registration Act of 1950 classified every South African by race. Other new laws prohibited interracial marriage or sexual intercourse. South Africans were segregated when using buses, taxis, cinemas, restaurants, hotels, trains, waiting rooms—even hearses.

The Group Areas Act of 1950 segregated both the residential and business areas of cities. The government forcibly removed thousands of coloreds and Indians from areas newly classified for whites only.

The Suppression of Communism Act of 1950 defined communism in extremely general terms. It gave government officials the right to detain anyone suspected of furthering communist aims. Police were later given the right to arrest and detain people without trial and without access to family or lawyers, and courts had virtually no way to intervene.

In 1951, the government abolished the Natives Representative Council. It forced Africans to live in the reserves except when working for whites. Pass laws made it illegal for Africans to be in a town for more than 72 hours without a job in a white home or business. The reserves were consolidated into first eight and then ten "homelands" of a specific African ethnic community. The government placed compliant chiefs in charge of the homelands.

The Bantu Education Act of 1953 took African schools away from the missions. Because of the demand for semiskilled black labor, the government created African schools that offered classes primarily in the lower grades. These schools had rigidly prescribed lessons. Textbooks endorsed official policies.

In 1956 the parliament removed the colored voters from the voting rolls. In return it allowed colored voters to elect four whites to represent them in the parliament. Three years later Africans lost the right to elect white representatives. Indians had never been represented in the parliament, and the colored voters lost their representation in 1969.

South Africa became a republic in 1961. Because other members of the British Commonwealth criticized its racial policies, South Africa withdrew from that association at about the same time.

In general, Afrikaners had a lower standard of living than did the British in South Africa. Determined to change that situation, the National Party advanced Afrikaners to top positions in the civil service, army, police, and state corporations.

REVITILIZATION OF RESISTANCE TO APARTHEID LAWS

Because of the apartheid laws, life became a struggle to survive for most nonwhites. Poverty, malnutrition, and disease became commonplace even though the South African economy was growing. But hardships also revitalized resistance movements. In 1952 ANC President Albert Lutuli and three younger men—Oliver Tambo, Nelson Mandela, and Walter Sisulu—working with the South African Indian Congress, organized a passive resistance campaign against the apartheid laws. In 1955 they held a mass meeting called the Congress of the People. The government broke up the meeting and arrested 156 people, charging them with high treason. No one was convicted, but the last prisoner wasn't released until 1961.

A group of Africans led by Robert Sobukwe broke off from the ANC in 1959 and founded the Pan-Africanist Congress (PAC). On March 21, 1960, thousands of unarmed Africans organized by the PAC appeared at police stations without passes. The police at Sharpeville opened fire. Most of the dead and wounded were shot in the back as they were running away.

This attack spurred thousands of African workers to go on strike. In Cape Town 30,000 Africans marched peacefully to the center of the city. The government responded by mobilizing the army, forcibly breaking up the demonstration, outlawing the ANC and the PAC, and arresting more than 11,000 people.

Because of these events, leaders in both the ANC and PAC concluded that violent action was necessary to bring an end to an illegitimate government. The resultant bombings and other violent acts had little effect. By 1964 most of their leadership had been arrested, including Mandela and Sobukwe. Hundreds of other ANC and PAC members fled the country, and Oliver Tambo presided over the exiled ANC in Zambia.

In 1973 black trade unions organized a series of strikes. At the same time Steve Biko founded a Black Consciousness movement designed to encourage Africans to take pride in their culture. That year the UN General Assembly declared apartheid to be "a crime against humanity."

Thousands of children in Soweto demonstrated on June 16, 1976. Police opened fire on the children. This sparked a year-long cycle of protests followed by repression. By the end of that year, 500 people had been killed, including Steve Biko. This round of violence captured the world's attention. In 1977 the UN Security Council unanimously established an embargo on the export of arms to South Africa. Opponents of apartheid, especially university students, began calling for boycotts of South African goods and pressuring their universities to sell off any stocks held in South African companies.

Changes were also taking place in South Africa. The National Party was coming under the control of younger, urban Afrikaners who were sensitive to world opinion and its effects on business. Many well-educated white South Africans were leaving the country, and its economy was declining.

The Elimination of Apartheid

The first step toward eliminating apartheid came when Pieter W. Botha became prime minister in 1978. His administration eliminated some apartheid laws, but Africans still couldn't vote and segregation still existed in housing. Nonwhites were extremely poor, and the healthcare and education they received were drastically inferior to those of whites. Botha also engaged in a massive military buildup.

Pressure from both blacks and whites in South Africa to end apartheid increased. In 1985 the Botha government responded by declaring a state of emergency. Over the next four years, thousands of Africans were tortured and killed by police. Censorship laws banned news of these events from South African media outlets.

Critics such as Archbishop Desmond Tutu spoke out against the Botha government, and many Afrikaner clergy and intellectuals stopped supporting Botha. Strikes by black workers and the continuing impact of sanctions caused the economy to falter. Inflation rose above 14 percent.

In 1986 U.S. public opinion against apartheid was so strong that Congress passed the Comprehensive Anti-Apartheid Act. It banned new investments in loans to South Africa and prohibited the importation of many South African goods. When President Ronald Reagan vetoed the bill, Congress overrode his veto. Other nations took similar action.

Leaders within the National Party held talks with Nelson Mandela, but Botha still refused to allow Africans to have any say in government. In 1989 he stepped down as party leader and was replaced by F. W. de Klerk. Mandela was released from prison, and in 1991 the South African parliament repealed the basic apartheid laws. Many political prisoners were freed, and those in exile were allowed to return.

DE KLERK'S AND MANDELA'S SEARCH FOR PEACE

Mandela succeeded Oliver Tambo as president of the ANC in 1991. De Klerk and Mandela held many meetings, trying to find a way to bring peace to their nation.

Representatives of most of the nation's political organizations met to create a new constitution. While these meetings took place, violence increased in the African townships. In Natal Zulu supporters of the ANC clashed with members of the Inkatha Freedom Party, a Zulu ethnic movement led by Chief Mangosuthu Buthelezi. In the Transvaal Zulu migrant workers fought with residents of neighboring townships.

Both Mandela and de Klerk made concessions that put them at risk of being rejected by their own constituents. Black and white extremists tried to sabotage the process of uniting South Africa. By the end of 1993, the leaders of 20 political parties endorsed a new constitution, which would take effect immediately after South Africa's first open election. That election, in April 1994, gave the ANC 63 percent of the vote, the National Party 20 percent, and the Inkatha Party 10 percent.

Mandela was sworn in as president of South Africa on May 10, 1994, and retired in 1999. His country still faces many challenges. From 1997 to 1999 a Truth and Reconciliation Commission investigated human rights violations committed between March 1, 1960 (a few weeks before the police shooting in Sharpeville) and May 10, 1994 (when Mandela became president). The controversial commission, led by Archbishop Desmond Tutu, attempted to deal with much of the pain in South Africa's past.

South Africa's future, however, still carries that pain. Inequalities in housing, education, healthcare, employment, and wealth persist. Political conflicts based on historical rivalries between African groups continue to be felt, and racist attitudes prevail in many quarters. In a land wealthy in natural resources, the dream of unity remains unfulfilled. For the first time in more than a century, however, its future rests in the hands of all its inhabitants.

CHRONOLOGY

1867	Diamonds are discovered in Griqualand West
1871	The British annex Griqualand West
1877	Theophilus Shepstone annexes the Transvaal
1879	Zulu War takes place
1880	Afrikaners revolt in the Transvaal
1886	Large gold deposits are discovered in the Witwatersrand area of the Transvaal
1888	Cecil Rhodes incorporates all his diamond mines under De Beers Consolidated Mines, Ltd.
1889	Rinderpest epidemic begins to spread through southern Africa, killing cattle; Rhodes forms British South Africa Company
1890	Plague of locusts strikes southern Africa
1894	Severe drought hits southern Africa
1895	Jameson Raid fails to create an internal uprising in the Transvaal
1899	South African War between Britain and the Afrikaners begins
1902	South African War ends with the Peace of Vereeniging on May 31; African Political Organization and South African Native Congress are founded
1906	Indians led by Gandhi hold mass protest against registration requirements in Natal; chief Bambatha leads African protest against poll tax in Natal
1908	Constitutional convention convenes in May
1909	South African Native Convention is held May 24–26; South African Act of Union is passed by British House of Commons
1910	Union of South Africa is established with four provinces on May 31
1912	African National Congress is founded in Bloemfontein
1913	Natives Land Act passes
1950	First of the apartheid laws passes
1961	Republic of South Africa is created; nation withdraws from the British Commonwealth
1994	Nelson Mandela is inaugurated as president of South Africa
1998	Report of South Africa's Truth and Reconciliation Commission, headed by Archbishop Desmond Tutu, released on October 29
1999	Nelson Mandela retires as president; Thabo Mbeki of the ANC becomes next president when his party wins a majority of the seats in parliament

GLOSSARY

Afrikaner—name given to descendants of Dutch immigrants to southern Africa.

Apartheid—a policy of segregation and discrimination against non-European people in South Africa. This policy was written into law beginning in 1950. Basic apartheid laws were repealed in 1991.

Bantu—a family of languages spoken in central and southern Africa, many of which share "clicking" noises.

Boer—Dutch word meaning "farmer." Originally used by Afrikaners to identify themselves, but such usage ended in the late 19th century when the British began using the term *Boer* as an insult.

Difaqane—Sesotho term meaning "the time of troubles" or "the forced migration"; used to describe Zulu attacks on neighboring African chiefdoms.

impi—a regiment of Zulu warriors.

Mfecane—a Zulu word meaning "the crushing"; used to describe attacks by Zulu warriors under Shaka and other leaders against neighboring African chiefdoms during the 1820s and 1830s. The *Mfecane* forced thousands of Africans to flee southeastern Africa.

protectorate—an arrangement whereby Great Britain took control of foreign relations and natural resources in a region. In exchange Britain promised to protect the people living there.

South African Act of Union—act passed by the British Parliament in 1909, which created the Union of South Africa.

South African War—war between Great Britain and the Afrikaners from 1899 to 1902. Called Second War of Freedom by Afrikaners and Boer War by British.

Uitlanders—literally, "outsider," an Afrikaner term used to describe non-Dutch immigrants in the Transvaal. These immigrants came from Europe, America, and other parts of Africa to get jobs in gold and diamond mining.

Zulu War—war in 1879 between Great Britain and the Zulu nation led by their king Cetshwayo.

WORLD WITHOUT END

DEIRDRE SHIELDS

ONE SUMMER'S DAY in 1830, a group of Englishmen met in London and decided to start a learned society to promote "that most important and entertaining branch of knowledge—Geography," and the Royal Geographical Society (RGS) was born.

The society was formed by the Raleigh Travellers' Club, an exclusive dining club, whose members met over exotic meals to swap tales of their travels. Members included Lord Broughton, who had travelled with the poet Byron, and John Barrow, who had worked in the iron foundries of Liverpool before becoming a force in the British Admiralty.

From the start, the Royal Geographical Society led the world in exploration, acting as patron and inspiration for the great expeditions to Africa, the Poles, and the Northwest Passage, that elusive sea connection between the Atlantic and Pacific. In the scramble to map the world, the society embodied the spirit of the age: that English exploration was a form of benign conquest.

The society's gold medal awards for feats of exploration read like a Who's Who of famous explorers, among them David Livingstone, for his 1855 explorations in Africa; the American explorer Robert Peary, for his 1898 discovery of the "northern termination of the Greenland ice"; Captain Robert Scott, the first Englishman to reach the South Pole, in 1912; and on and on.

Today the society's headquarters, housed in a red-brick Victorian lodge in South Kensington, still has the effect of a gentleman's club, with courteous staff, polished wood floors, and fine paintings.

WORLD WITHOUT END

The building archives the world's most important collection of private exploration papers, maps, documents, and artifacts. Among the RGS's treasures are the hats Livingstone and Henry Morton Stanley wore at their famous meeting ("Dr. Livingstone, I presume?") at Ujiji in 1871, and the chair the dying Livingstone was carried on during his final days in Zambia. The collection also includes models of expedition ships, paintings, dug-out canoes, polar equipment, and Charles Darwin's pocket sextant.

The library's 500,000 images cover the great moments of exploration. Here is Edmund Hillary's shot of Sherpa Tenzing standing on Everest. Here is Captain Lawrence Oates, who deliberately walked out of his tent in a blizzard to his death because his illness threatened to delay Captain Scott's party. Here, too is the American Museum of Natural History's 1920 expedition across the Gobi Desert in dusty convoy (the first to drive motorized vehicles across a desert).

The day I visited, curator Francis Herbert was trying to find maps for five different groups of adventurers at the same time from the largest private map collection in the world. Among the 900,000 items are maps dating to 1482 and ones showing the geology of the moon and thickness of ice in Antarctica, star atlases, and "secret" topographic maps from the former Soviet Union.

The mountaineer John Hunt pitched a type of base camp in a room at the RGS when he organized the 1953 Everest expedition that put Hillary and Tenzing on top of the world. "The society was my base, and source of my encouragement," said the late Lord Hunt, who noted that the nature of that work is different today from what it was when he was the society's president from 1976 to 1980. "When I was involved, there was still a lot of genuine territorial exploration to be done. Now, virtually every important corner—of the land surface, at any rate—has been discovered, and exploration has become more a matter of detail, filling in the big picture."

The RGS has shifted from filling in blanks on maps to providing a lead for the new kind of exploration, under the banner of geography: "I see exploration not so much as a question of 'what' and 'where' anymore, but 'why' and 'how': How does the earth work, the environment function, and how do we manage our resources sustainably?" says the society's director, Dr. Rita Gardner. "Our role today is to answer such questions at the senior level of scientific research," Gardner continues, "through our big, multidisciplinary expeditions, through the smaller expeditions we support and encourage, and by advancing the subject of geography, advising governments, and encouraging wider public understanding. Geography is the subject of the 21st century because it embraces everything—peoples, cultures, landscapes, environments—and pulls them all together."

The society occupies a unique position in world-class exploration. To be invited to speak at the RGS is still regarded as an accolade, the ultimate seal of approval of Swan, who in 1989 became the first person to walk to both the North and South Poles, and who says, "The hairs still stand on the back of my neck when I think about the first time I spoke at the RGS. It was the greatest honour."

The RGS set Swan on the path of his career as an explorer, assisting him with a 1979 expedition retracing Scott's journey to the South Pole. "I was a Mr. Nobody, trying to raise seven million dollars, and getting nowhere," says Swan. "The RGS didn't tell me I was mad—they gave me access to Scott's private papers. From those, I found fifty sponsors who had supported Scott, and persuaded them to fund me. On the basis of a photograph I found of one of his chaps sitting on a box of 'Shell Spirit,' I got Shell to sponsor the fuel for my ship."

The name "Royal Geographical Society" continues to open doors. Although the society's actual membership—some 12,600 "fellows," as they are called—is small, the organization offers an incomparable network of people, experience, and expertise. This is seen in the work of the Expeditionary Advisory Centre. The EAC was established in 1980 to provide a focus for would-be explorers. If you want to know how to raise sponsorship, handle snakes safely, or find a mechanic for your trip across the Sahara, the EAC can help. Based in Lord Hunt's old Everest office, the EAC funds some 50 small expeditions a year and offers practical training and advice to hundreds more. Its safety tips range from the pragmatic—"In subzero temperatures, metal spectacle frames can cause frostbite (as can earrings and nose-rings)"—to the unnerving—"Remember: A decapitated snake head can still bite."

The EAC is unique, since it is the only center in the world that helps small-team, low-budget expeditions, thus keeping the amateur—in the best sense of the word—tradition of exploration alive.

WORLD WITHOUT END

"The U.K. still sends out more small expeditions per capita than any other country," says Dr. John Hemming, director of the RGS from 1975 to 1996. During his tenure, Hemming witnessed the growth in exploration-travel. "In the 1960s we'd be dealing with 30 to 40 expeditions a year. By 1997 it was 120, but the quality hadn't gone down—it had gone up. It's a boom time for exploration, and the RGS is right at the heart of it."

While the EAC helps adventure-travelers, it concentrates its funding on scientific field research projects, mostly at the university level. Current projects range from studying the effect of the pet trade on Madagscar's chameleons, to mapping uncharted terrain in the south Ecuadorian cloud forest. Jen Hurst is a typical "graduate" of the EAC. With two fellow Oxford students, she received EAC technical training, support, and a $2,000 grant to do biological surveys in the Kyabobo Range, a new national park in Ghana.

"The RGS's criteria for funding are very strict," says Hurst. "They put you through a real grilling, once you've made your application. They're very tough on safety, and very keen on working alongside people from the host country. The first thing they wanted to be sure of was whether we would involve local students. They're the leaders of good practice in the research field."

When Hurst and her colleagues returned from Ghana in 1994, they presented a case study of their work at an EAC seminar. Their talk prompted a $15,000 award from the BP oil company for them to set up a registered charity, the Kyabobo Conservation Project, to ensure that work in the park continues and that followup ideas for community-based conservation, social, and education projects are developed. "It's been a great experience, and crucial to the careers we hope to make in environmental work," says Hurst, age 24. "And it all started through the RGS."

The RGS is rich in prestige but it is not particularly wealthy in financial terms. Compared to the National Geographic Society in the U.S., the RGS is a pauper. However, bolstered by sponsorship from such companies as British Airways and Discovery Channel Europe, the RGS remains one of Britain's largest organizers of geographical field research overseas.

The ten major projects the society has undertaken over the last 20 or so years have spanned the world, from Pakistan and Oman to Brunei, and Australia. The scope is large—hundreds of people are currently working in the field, and the emphasis is multidisciplinary, with the aim to break down traditional barriers, not only among the different strands of science but also among nations. This is exploration as The Big Picture, preparing blueprints for governments around the globe to work on. For example, the 1977 Mulu (Sarawak) expedition to Borneo was credited with kick-starting the international concern for tropical rain forests.

The society's three current projects include water and soil erosion studies in Nepal, sustainable land use in Jordan, and a study of the Mascarene Plateau in the western Indian Ocean, to develop ideas on how best to conserve ocean resources in the future.

Projects adhere to a strict code of procedure. "The society works only at the invitation of host governments and in close cooperation with local people," explains Winser. "The findings are published in the host countries first, so they can get the benefit. Ours are long-term projects, looking at processes and trends, adding to the sum of existing knowledge, which is what exploration is about."

Exploration has never been more fashionable in England. More people are traveling adventurously on their own account, and the RGS's increasingly younger membership (the average age has dropped in the last 20 years from over 45 to the early 30s) is exploration-literate and able to make the fine distinctions between adventure / extreme / expedition / scientific travel.

Rebecca Stephens, who in 1993 became the first British woman to summit Everest, says she "pops along on Monday evenings to listen to the lectures." These occasions are sociable, informal affairs, where people find themselves talking to such luminaries as explorer Sir Wilfred Thesiger, who attended Haile Selassie's coronation in Ethiopia in 1930, or David Puttnam, who produced the film *Chariots of Fire* and is a vice president of the RGS. Shortly before his death, Lord Hunt was spotted in deep conversation with the singer George Michael.

Summing up the society's enduring appeal, Shane Winser says, "The Royal Geographical Society is synonymous with exploration, which is seen as something brave and exciting. In a sometimes dull, depressing world, the Royal Geographical Society offers a spirit of adventure people are always attracted to."

FURTHER READING

AFRICA NEWS on the World Wide Web at **http://www.africanews.org**.

African National Congress webpage at **http://www.anc.org**.

Alvyn, Austin, "Discovering Livingstone," *Christian History,* issue 56, at **http://www. christianity.net/christianhistory/56H/56H010.**

Boonzaier, Emile, ed. *The Cape Herders: A History of the Khoikhoi of Southern Africa.* Athens, Ohio: Ohio University Press, 1998.

Encyclopaedia Britannica Online at **http://www.eb.com**.

Meredith, Martin. *Nelson Mandela: A Biography.* New York: St. Martin's Press, 1998.

Morris, Donald R. *The Washing of the Spears: A History of the Rise of the Zulu Nation Under Shaka and Its Fall in the Zulu War of 1879.* New York: Da Capo Press, 1998.

Mostert, Noël. *Frontiers: The Epic of South Africa's Creation and the Tragedy of the Xhosa People.* New York: Random House, 1992.

Pakenham, Thomas. *The Boer War.* New York: Random House, 1979.

Pakenham, Thomas. *The Scramble for Africa: White Man's Conquest of the Dark Continent from 1876 to 1912.* New York: Avon, 1992.

South African War Virtual Library webpage at **http://www.up.net.au/~zzrwotto/contents**.

South Africa Truth and Reconciliation Commission. *Truth and Reconciliation Commission of South Africa Report,* 5 vols. New York: Grove's Dictionaries, 1999.

Thompson, Leonard. *A History of South Africa.* New Haven, Conn.: Yale University Press, 1990.

Wilson, Monica, and Leonard Thompson, eds. *The Oxford History of South Africa,* 2 vols. New York: Oxford University Press, 1969–1971.

INDEX

ABOUT THE AUTHORS

Dr. Richard E. Leakey is a distinguished paleo-anthropologist and conservationist. He is chairman of the Wildlife Clubs of Kenya Association and the Foundation for the Research into the Origins of Man. He presented the BBC-TV series *The Making of Mankind* (1981) and wrote the accompanying book. His other publications include *People of the Lake* (1979) and *One Life* (1984). Richard Leakey, along with his famous parents, Louis and Mary, was named by *Time* magazine as one of the greatest minds of the twentieth century.

Bruce and Becky Durost Fish are freelance writers and editors who have worked on more than one hundred books for children and young adults, including *Benjamin Franklin* and *The History of the Democratic Party* in the COLONIAL LEADERS and YOUR GOVERNMENT series respectively.

Deirdre Shields is the author of many articles dealing with contemporary life in Great Britain. Her essays have appeared in *The Times*, *The Daily Telegraph*, *Harpers & Queen*, and *The Field*.